HEALTH FOR THE PACIFIC 8

Puberty, Reproduction and Sexuality

in Papua New Guinea

Richard Jones and Jennifer Miller

OXFORD
UNIVERSITY PRESS
AUSTRALIA & NEW ZEALAND

Oxford University Press is a department of the University of Oxford.
It furthers the University's objective of excellence in research,
scholarship, and education by publishing worldwide. Oxford is a registered
trademark of Oxford University Press in the UK and in certain other countries.

Published in Australia by
Oxford University Press
Level 8, 737 Bourke Street, Docklands, Victoria 3008, Australia

First published 2011

Reprinted 2023 (D)

ISBN 978 0 19 557598 9

Typeset by Leigh Ashforth
Illustrated by Dimitrios Prokopis, Paul Konye and Rob Mancini
Proofread by Emma Short
Printed and bound in Australia by Ligare Book Printers Pty Ltd

The author and the publisher wish to thank the following copyright holders for reproduction of their material.

Corbis/Anders Ryman, p.40 (bottom left); iStock Photo/Eduardo Luzzatti Buyé, p.78 (IUD); photolibrary/Goran Burenhult, p.40 (top) /MIG TIPS RF, p.40 (bottom right); Shutterstock/ T. Kimmeskamp, p.64 (bottom) /liseykina, p.64 (top) /sarah2, p.78 (contraceptive pills) /design56, p.78 (contraceptive injection); Wikimedia Commons/Ceridwen, p.78 (female condom).

Every effort has been made to trace the original source of copyright material contained in this book. The publisher will be pleased to hear from copyright holders to rectify any errors or omissions.

Contents

Foreword iv

Acknowledgments iv

Notes for teachers v

Introduction vii

Chapter 1	The stages of life	1
Chapter 2	What is puberty?	3
Chapter 3	Becoming an adult	6
Chapter 4	A girl's guide to healthy puberty	15
Chapter 5	A boy's guide to healthy puberty	27
Chapter 6	Healthy sexuality	34
Chapter 7	Love, relationships and marriage	41
Chapter 8	Sexual intercourse and sexual pleasure	46
Chapter 9	Safe and healthy sex	54
Chapter 10	Reproduction, fertilisation and pregnancy	62
Chapter 11	Parenthood and family planning	73
Chapter 12	Where can I find the right information?	82

Glossary 86

Foreword

The *Health for the Pacific* series aims to educate young men and women about important health issues that are affecting their lives.

During puberty and into early adulthood, young people experience physical and emotional changes as well as changes in their social roles and responsibilities. In the Pacific, puberty and topics related to sex and sexuality are often taboo, and it can be very difficult for young people to get correct information. Lack of information and poor understanding about these changes can make this a confusing and difficult time for young people. It is important that young people understand these changes and their impact for healthy physical and personal development.

This book aims to give a simple, accurate and interesting introduction to puberty and sexual and reproductive health for young people.

Acknowledgments

Learning about puberty, sexuality and sexual and reproductive health is an important part of educating young people and contributing to their personal development. The text is written to support the teaching of Health and Personal Development in Papua New Guinea primary and secondary schools from Grade 5 onwards. It is a textbook for students and a resource book for teachers.

We would like to thank the many dedicated teachers and health workers who teach about the body and how to look after it, and who help guide young people through the changes and challenges in their lives. We were taught to be curious and respectful of and amazed by the human body by our teachers and parents. We dedicate this book to teachers, and to our parents – Joan, Jenny, Bill and Robin.

Richard Jones and Jennifer Miller

Notes for teachers

This textbook is written to be used by Primary and Lower Secondary students and their teachers.

The knowledge, skills and attitudes in the text develop these learning outcomes from the Health and Personal Development subjects in Papua New Guinea.

Health Grade 5

5.1.1 Identify changes that occur during puberty and propose actions to promote health and growth

Personal Development Grades 6–8

6.4.1 Describe the stages in growth and development and the health needs at various stages

6.4.2 Explore influences of inherited characteristics and environmental factors on growth and development

6.4.3 Investigate various sources of information about sexual development

7.4.1 Explore the functions of different systems and parts of the body

7.4.2 Describe physical, social and emotional changes in both boys and girls during puberty

8.4.1 Identify and describe behaviour that promotes growth and development, taking into account heredity and environment

8.4.2 Outline issues arising from differences in rates of growth and development and how individuals manage the changes

8.4.3 Identify different cultural beliefs and values about sexuality

8.4.7 Discuss safe sexual behaviour and sexual responsibilities

Personal Development Grades 9–10

9.3.2 Describe ways to deal with sexual health safely during adolescence including avoiding HIV and AIDS

10.1.1 Explain the functions of the male and female reproductive anatomy with respect to conception and pregnancy

10.1.2 Explain the relationship between family size and family welfare

10.1.3 Compare and contrast the effectiveness of a range of decision-making skills and conflict resolution skills in regard to sexual issues

There are many activities in the text for the students to complete and discuss. These can be used for self-study or as teaching and learning activities in class. They are designed for maximum student participation and developing life skills.

Introduction

Puberty is a time of many changes for young people as they move from childhood to adulthood. The physical changes of puberty are combined with changing roles in relationships, families and communities. When young people are given the correct information about puberty, reproduction and sexuality they are more likely to respect their bodies, understand the changes and develop healthy behaviour and attitudes.

In the past, young people in PNG learned about puberty, reproduction and sexuality through their elders when they reached puberty. These days, there are many factors that have led to changing cultural traditions, and there is often no opportunity for young people to learn about their changing bodies and how to develop and manage their sexuality safely in and out of marriage.

Adolescence can be a time of risk for young men and young women. Many young people learn about puberty, sex and sexuality from their peers, parents, teachers, TV, movies, magazines, church and initiation ceremonies. Often these messages can be different from one another and cause confusion.

How you experience puberty and the many changes associated with puberty is unique to you, but all human beings experience puberty and have the same sexual and reproductive systems. Understanding the changes that take place during puberty will make it a less confusing experience and contribute to healthy and responsible sexual behaviour. This book will explain the many changes that take place during this time.

Chapter 1 The stages of life

Human beings grow, develop and change throughout their lives. In your community there are people at every stage of the human life cycle. As humans grow older they change physically, emotionally, spiritually and socially. Their roles and responsibilities change, too. We are all unique individuals, even though many of the changes we experience are changes all humans go through.

Puberty is one of the most important changes in your life. It marks the change from being a child to becoming an adult. Every person experiences puberty.

The stages of life

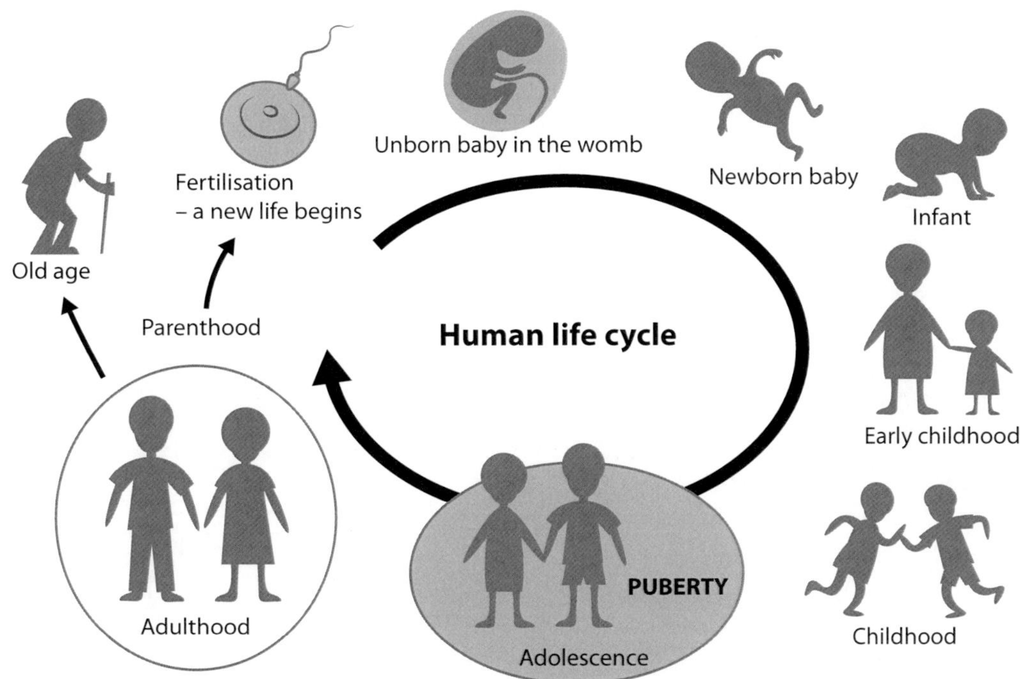

Activity 1·1 CHANGES

What are the differences between each stage in the human life cycle? Think about how a person at each stage would spend their day.

- Where do they live?
- Who do they live with?
- Who prepares their meals?
- Who do they talk to?
- What responsibilities do they have?
- What are the physical signs that someone is that age?

Activity 1·2 TEACHING ABOUT PUBERTY, SEXUALITY AND REPRODUCTION

With a group of same-sex peers, discuss these questions.

1 Why is it important that young men and women learn about puberty and sexual health in schools?

2 What are some of the challenges to learning about puberty and sexual health in school?

3 How can these challenges be overcome? What recommendations would you make to your teachers?

4 What do you think are the most important things to learn about puberty and sexual health?

Chapter 2 What is puberty?

Puberty is a time of many changes for young men and women. It is the change from childhood to adolescence and then to adulthood.

During this time, young people develop their personalities, life skills, independence and values that give them their unique identities.

Young people are faced with many decisions about school, employment, family and relationships during this time. The more you know about what happens and what to do during puberty, the better you will be able to enjoy growing up and developing into a healthy and responsible adult.

The changes of puberty

By the time the physical changes of puberty are complete, your body will be able to make children through sexual intercourse. However, the emotional, social and intellectual changes continue for some years as you mature into an adult. This longer period is called **adolescence.**

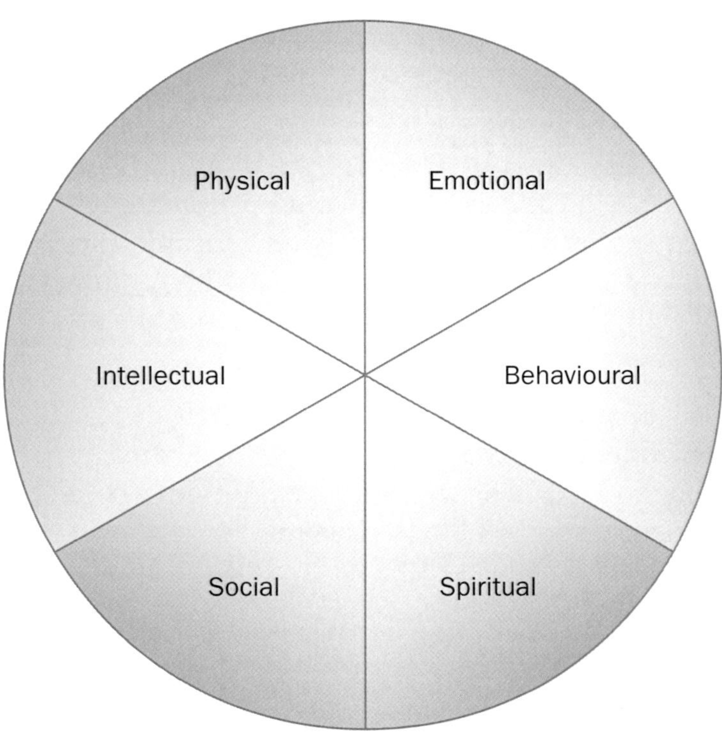

When does puberty begin?

For most girls the physical changes of puberty begin around the age of 11 years old, but some girls start puberty younger and some girls' bodies don't start changing until they are 14 or 15. Almost all girls finish puberty by the age of 17.

Boys usually start puberty later than girls. For most boys the physical changes of puberty begin around the age of 13 years old but some boys start puberty when they are younger and some start when they are older. Almost all boys finish the physical changes of puberty by the age of 18.

At the end of puberty, young men and women will be able to produce children. Their reproductive system will be developed and they will experience sexual feelings and sexual pleasure and be able to **orgasm**.

Young men will begin making **sperm** and young women will start **menstruating** and releasing an **egg** every month. Their bodies will change into adult bodies, becoming stronger and taller.

The physical changes of puberty begin at different times for each boy and girl. This can be a concern for some boys and girls. However, this is natural.

Activity 2·1 PUBERTY – IT IS NOT A RACE!

Dear Agony Uncle,

I am worried. All my friends have started growing beards and pubic hair. I am the smallest in my group and have not started shaving yet! Help!

1 What advice would you give this student?
2 How could you help your younger brothers or sisters or younger students prepare for puberty? What information do they need?

What causes puberty?

The changes at puberty are controlled by **hormones**. Hormones are chemical messengers that cause physical and emotional changes in the body. Hormones for puberty are produced in the pituitary gland in the brain as well as in the male and female reproductive organs (**testes** and **ovaries**).

Chapter 3 Becoming an adult

Not all of the changes at puberty are physical. As you grow up, you start to develop a sense of who you are and what makes you unique. You develop a set of beliefs and values, interests and goals. These emotional, intellectual, social, spiritual and behavioural changes take place over many years. Many factors influence this development.

Emotional development

People can experience many different feelings. Some feelings are good and happy, but others are harmful and unhappy. One important emotion that develops during puberty is sexual attraction. This is a powerful feeling which needs self-control.

It is normal for young people's emotions to change dramatically from one day to the next, or even from one minute to the next. This is called a mood swing.

Mood swings can be frustrating for the young person as well as for their friends and family. With time and support, most young people will learn different ways of coping with their changing moods.

Managing strong emotions

Angry or excited people do not always make good judgments and this can lead to problems. Most people have seen someone lose their temper. Being able to stop and think calmly could keep you safe. These skills help you to maintain healthy relationships with others.

Activity 3·1 STAYING COOL

1 This young man is very angry at his family. What advice would you give to him? (For example, count to ten before speaking, walking away and cooling off.)
2 Could his family have done anything to prevent his anger?
3 Think of a time in your family when someone did not control their emotions. What happened? How could they have acted? What should the other people do?
4 What are the dangers of losing self-control when you are feeling a strong emotion of sexual attraction and desire towards someone?

Intellectual development

As young people grow up, they also develop better mental skills. They learn to look critically at different situations and make better judgments. This is the life skill of decision making.

We also learn which sources of information can be trusted and how to tell when we are being misled or lied to.

Activity 3·2 DECISIONS, DECISIONS

Case study 1

You are at school. It is the end of the day. Two students from your class are bullying a younger girl.

1 What would be a mature decision? What would you do? Why?

2 What would be a poor decision? Why?

Case study 2

An older man who has a good job in town asks you to a hotel. He is an uncle with plenty of money. You think he might want something for the money ...

3 What would be a mature decision? What would you do? Why?

4 What would be a poor decision? Why?

5 Now write a decision-making case study for a friend to solve.

Activity 3·3 OPINIONS

During puberty we start to develop our own opinions about the world.

What are your opinions about these issues? Do you think your opinions would ever change?

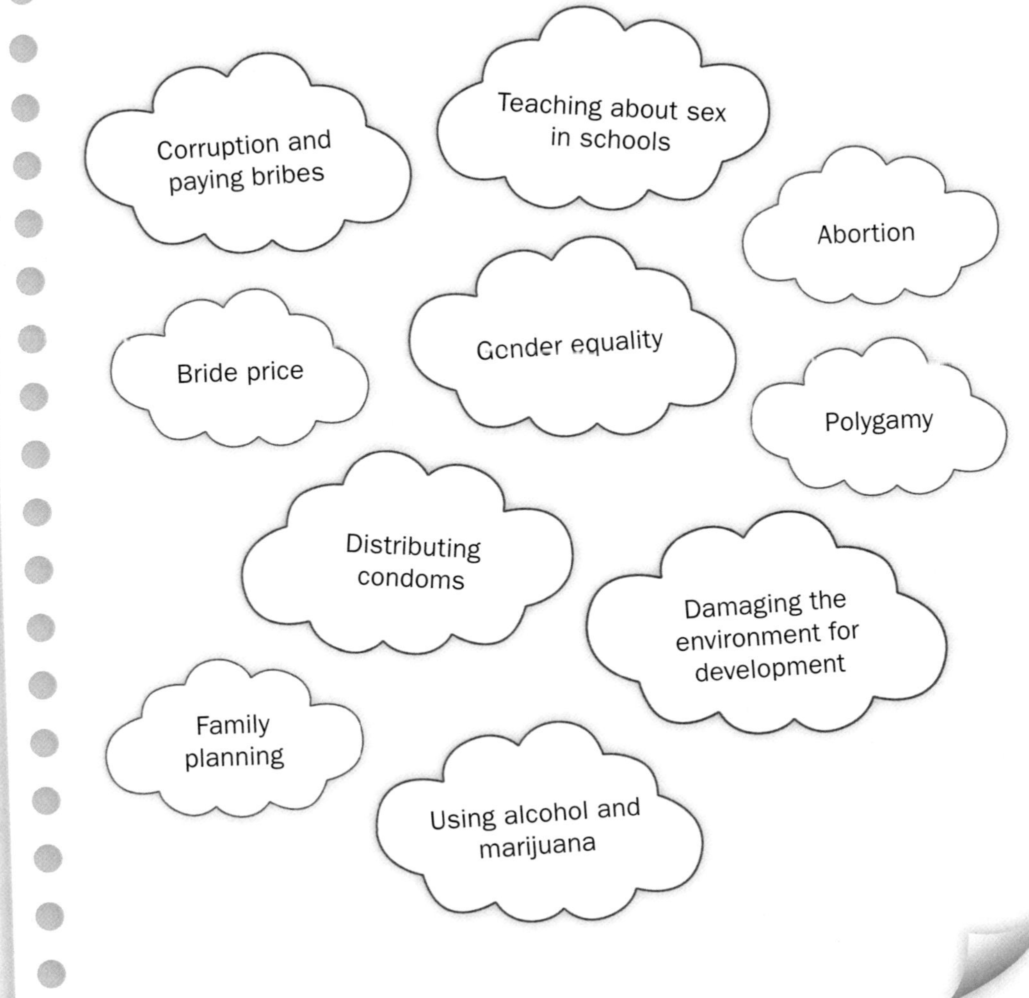

Developing values

Our values may change as we get older and more experienced. Meeting people from other cultures, reading about the world, religious beliefs and developing different relationships all shape our values.

We base our opinions on our values and experiences.

Activity 3·4 EXPLORING VALUES

1. Write a list of your values. For example, *respecting others, fairness.*
2. Now try to sort this list into which values are the *most* important to you. Why?
3. Finally, select one of the issues in Activity 3.3 and compare your opinion to that of your friend.
   - Do you agree with your friend's values on this issue?
   - Now compare what you and your friends think with what your parents and grandparents think. What do you notice?

Social development

As young people go through puberty, their relationships with their friends, family and communities start to change. They develop more friendships and relationships outside of their families and become more independent.

Young people will start to value the opinions of their friends, peers and role models, rather than the opinions of older family or community members.

Some of these new relationships will be romantic with feelings of sexual attraction towards others. There is more information on this in Chapter 7.

Along with these changing relationships, adolescents also have changing roles and responsibilities. They will often be expected to work and study and can take on important roles in families and in schools. These are all signs of increasing independence.

Cultural development

In many Pacific cultures there are events to mark the change from childhood to adulthood. These can be secret initiations or public celebrations. Often the type of ceremony depends on whether the person is a boy or a girl. The timing of this 'coming of age' ceremony can also vary. For example, sometimes a ceremony is held when a girl has her first period.

Initiation is an important tradition in many places. Young people are taught about their culture, taught how to behave and given information about relationships and marriage.

Cultural ceremonies include:

- special work (such as working in the garden or making a canoe)
- tattooing
- scar cutting
- dances and singsings
- learning secrets from uncles or aunties
- male circumcision or cutting the skin of the penis
- entering the haus man or haus meri for the first time.

Activity 3·5 'COMING OF AGE' CEREMONIES

1. Ask a trusted elder in your community or family about the 'coming of age' ceremony in your culture. Please respect any secrecy taboos.
   - Does it still happen?
   - When does it happen?
   - Who organises it?
   - What happens during it?
   - How are the young people different after it?
2. Think about health during 'coming of age' ceremonies.
   - **a** Are there any risks to the health of the young person because of the ceremony? For example, during skin cutting.
   - **b** How can these risks be prevented?
   - **c** What health information do you think young men and young women learn in their initiation?

Spiritual development

Adolescents often have many questions about the world and their place in it. Puberty can be a time for exploring how you feel about God, church and religion.

Values and beliefs will be tested, questioned and developed as young people become more independent and experiment with many parts of their lives. Spiritual beliefs can also be a good moral guide during all of these changes.

Activity 3·6 HELPING OTHERS

Many young people start to take more responsibility in helping others and contributing to community life in the home, school and church.

1 How will you contribute to your community today? Write down at least three positive actions you will take and carry them out.

The universal values of love, respect, tolerance, honesty and care for others are essential for human development.

2 Reflect on these values and your beliefs. Write either a prayer for young people or a poem of advice for young people based on these important values.

Behavioural development

As young people grow up they start to experiment with different behaviours. This helps young people to discover who they are and what they like and helps develop their identity.

Sometimes experimentation can lead to risky behaviours. It is important for young people to know their own strengths and weaknesses and to trust in their values. They must consider the consequences of their decisions so that they can make healthy life choices.

Activity 3·7 RISKY BEHAVIOUR AND EXPERIMENTS

Young people often experiment with different behaviours during puberty. These behaviours include:

- drinking alcohol
- cult activity in school
- generation names
- smoking tobacco
- smoking marijuana
- having sex
- arguing with parents and teachers.

1 Discuss these behaviours with friends. What are the risks for young men and young women as a result of these behaviours? How can we support our friends to stay safe and healthy?

2 What other behaviours do you see in your community that increase risks for young people?

Chapter 4 A girl's guide to healthy puberty

There are many physical changes that happen during puberty. These changes happen over a period of time and start at different times for different girls. By the end of puberty, girls will have become adult women.

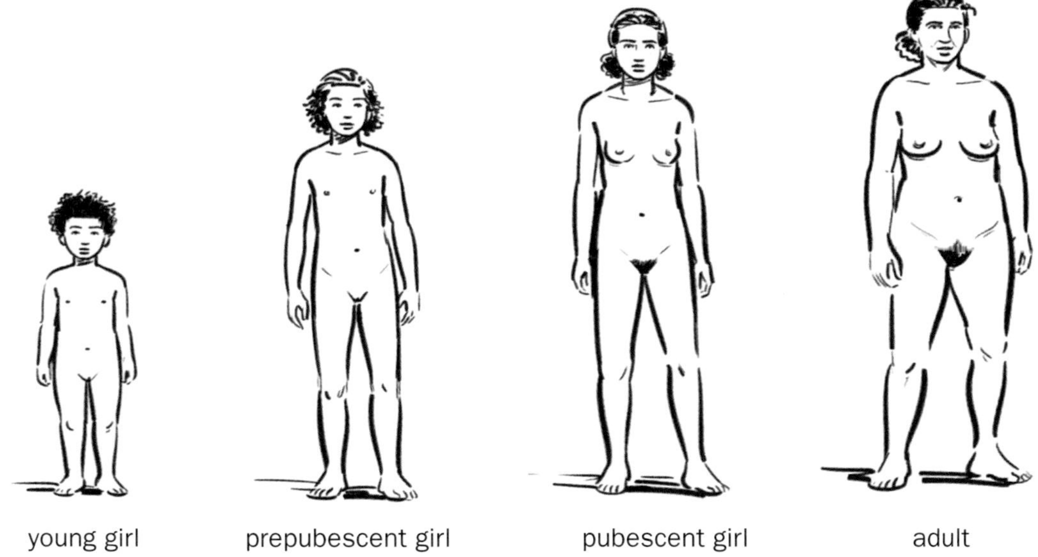

young girl prepubescent girl pubescent girl adult

These are some of the physical changes that happen to a girl during puberty:

- She grows taller and stronger.
- Her breasts grow and her nipples become larger.
- Her pubic hair grows.
- Hair grows under her arms.
- She begins ovulation and menstruation (a monthly period).
- She develops sexual feelings and the ability to orgasm.
- She has increased wetness in the vaginal area.
- Perspiration (sweat) increases.
- Some women get a line of hair on their belly and sometimes some hair on their face.

Female reproductive system

You should not feel shy or embarrassed about learning and talking about the different parts of the reproductive system. Being able to talk about your reproductive system easily with health workers or sexual partners is an important part of developing into a healthy and responsible adult.

The internal female reproductive organs

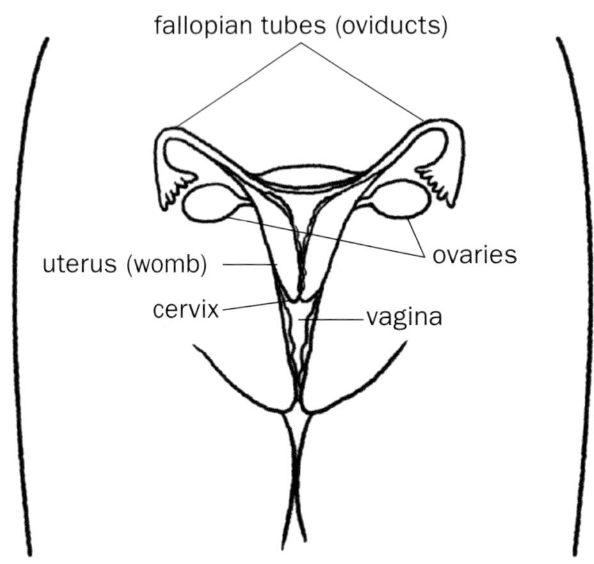

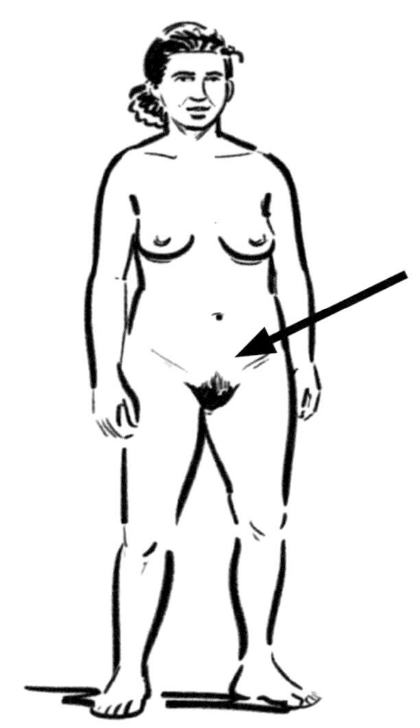

The female reproductive system is mostly hidden inside a woman's body. This is so that her body can protect the eggs and, later, a growing baby.

The functions of the parts of the female reproductive system are listed in the Glossary at the back of the book.

The external female reproductive organs

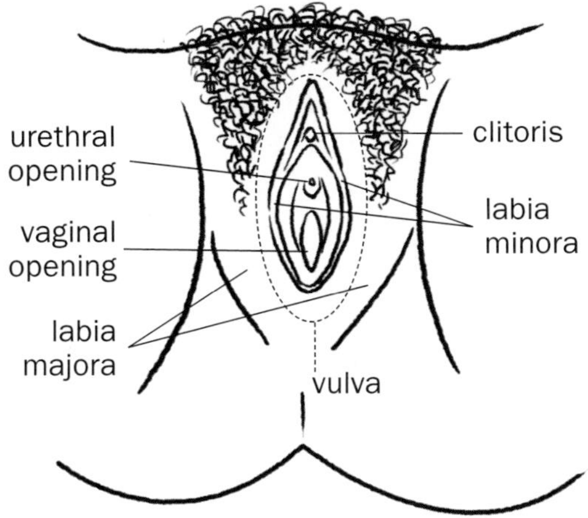

You can read more about the reproductive system in the *Health for the Pacific: Body Systems* book.

Menstruation

The biggest physical change for a girl is that she starts menstruation. For several days each month, menstrual blood and tissue comes out of a woman's vagina. This is called a 'period'. It is normal and healthy and is a sign that a girl is becoming a woman.

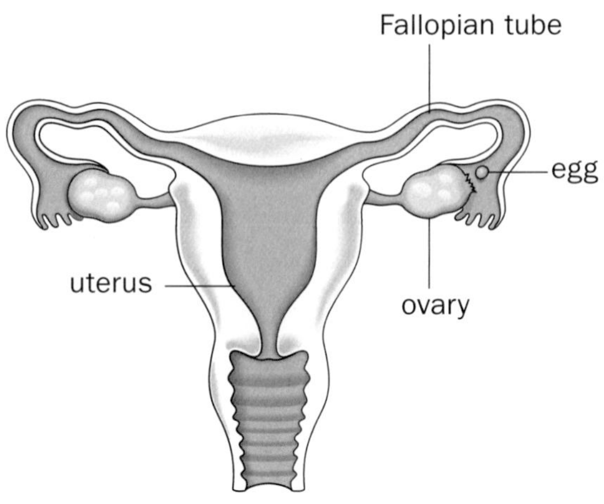

1 Girls are born with thousands of tiny eggs in their two ovaries. Each month one egg becomes ready and leaves the ovary. This is called ovulation.

The egg starts to float down the Fallopian tube.

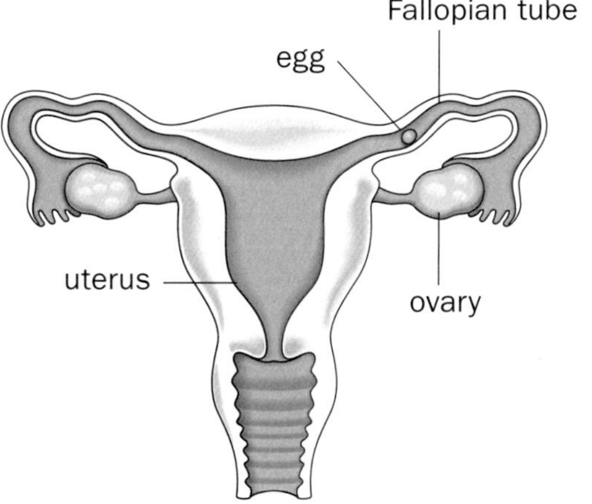

2 The egg travels down the Fallopian tube towards the uterus.

During this time the woman can become pregnant.

At the same time, the wall of the uterus becomes thicker. If the egg is fertilised by a sperm, a new baby will develop in the uterus.

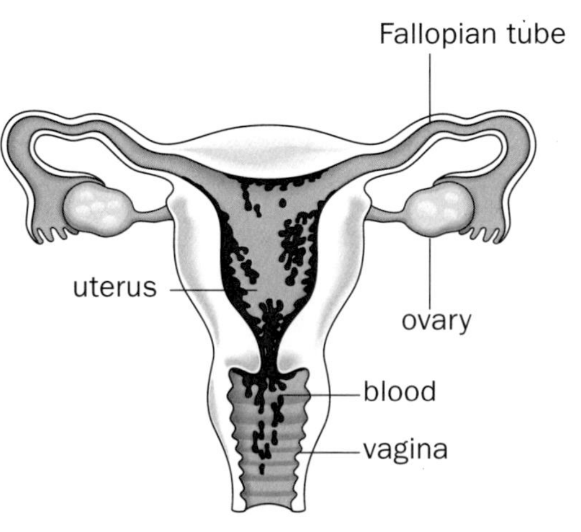

3 If the egg is not fertilised by a sperm, the lining of the uterus and the egg comes out of the vagina as menstrual blood. This is called a period. It happens about two weeks after ovulation.

After reaching puberty a woman produces one egg every three to five weeks.

The first time that a girl gets her period can be an emotional and confusing time. If she understands about periods and what to do when she gets her period, this will be a more positive experience for her.

These are some common questions asked by girls about periods.

How old are girls when they get their periods?

Most girls start their periods at around 12 or 13 years of age. Each girl is different, though, and it is not unusual for girls to start their periods as young as 10 or as old as 16 years of age. A girl's period will start when her body is ready. She does not have to do anything to make it start.

How will I know when I get my period?

A woman knows when she has started her period because a small amount of blood will come out of her vagina. Usually, she will feel the unusual wetness.

How long do periods last?

Periods last between three and seven days. It is different for each woman.

How often do women get their periods?

From the time a woman gets her first period, she will have a period each month. The time between one period and the next, or the length of a woman's menstrual cycle, is different for each woman. For most women the menstrual cycle is between 21 and 35 days.

I just started getting my period, but it doesn't come every month. Is there something wrong?

It is common for girls who are just starting to get their periods to have an irregular cycle. This means that their period may come each month or it may skip a month. This is normal.

There are many changes taking place in a growing girl's body, and it may take time for her body to adjust to all of these changes. As the girl grows older, her periods will become more regular.

How much blood will there be?

The amount of blood that comes out of the vagina is different for each woman. Most women will lose only a few spoonfuls of blood during a period.

The amount and colour of blood changes during my period. Is this normal?

It is normal for both the amount of blood and the colour of blood to change during a period. It is common for blood flow to be heavier at the start of a period. It is also common for the blood colour to change from dark red to a brownish colour.

When I have my period, do I have to stop doing things I enjoy?

When a woman has her period, she can do everything that she normally does. She can go to school, spend time with friends, play sports and do all of the things that she enjoys.

What should I do if I miss a period?

When a girl starts to get her period, it means that she can become pregnant. When a woman becomes pregnant, she will stop menstruating. Her periods will start again after she has a baby. If you have had vaginal sex and you miss a period, pregnancy is the most common reason. You should see a health worker and have a pregnancy test.

Can I get pregnant now my periods have started?

Yes. However, this does not mean that you are emotionally, mentally or socially ready to start a family or have a sexual relationship. There are many things that you need to experience and learn before you are mature enough to have a relationship or have children.

- For women between 45 and 50 years of age, missing a period could be a sign of **menopause**.
- At menopause, women's bodies experience another change and they are no longer able to ovulate. This means that they can no longer have children.
- This is a natural part of a woman's life cycle.

Activity 4·1 TALK TO YOUR SISTERS, MUM AND AUNTIES

All women get periods and all women's periods are different. There is no need for girls to experience puberty alone.

Talk to your family and older peers about their experiences.

1 How old were they when they first got their period?
2 How did they feel?
3 How did they keep themselves clean and healthy during their period?

Keeping healthy through your period

It is important for girls to take proper care to keep clean. During your periods, you should wash regularly. You should wash your entire body with soap each day. You should be careful not to use soap inside your vagina as this may cause irritation or infection.

Adolescents should drink plenty of clean water and eat a healthy diet that includes beans, green vegetables, meat and fish to replace iron that is lost in the blood during their periods.

During menstruation, it is important for girls to use something to absorb the blood as it leaves the vagina. Girls have several different options to choose from and these are described on the following page.

Whichever method you decide to use, you should change the item often. This will help to avoid stains, unpleasant smells and infections. Remember to always wash your hands before and afterwards.

Toilet paper

You can use clean toilet paper to make a thick, long pad and fit this inside your underwear. You should take care that pieces of the toilet paper do not come away and stay in the vagina, as this can cause infection.

Sanitary pads

These are disposable cotton pads bought in a store or pharmacy. They have strips of sticky tape to stick the pad to your underwear. Used pads should be disposed of carefully. They can be thrown down a pit latrine, buried or burnt. They should not be left in the garbage pile or flushed down the toilet.

Homemade cotton pads

You can use any clean material that easily soaks up liquid, such as old T-shirts and towels. You can cut and sew several layers of cloth together and fit this inside your underwear. These should be changed every few hours. You should clean them with unperfumed soap, salt or lemon juice and dry them well in the sun.

Tampons

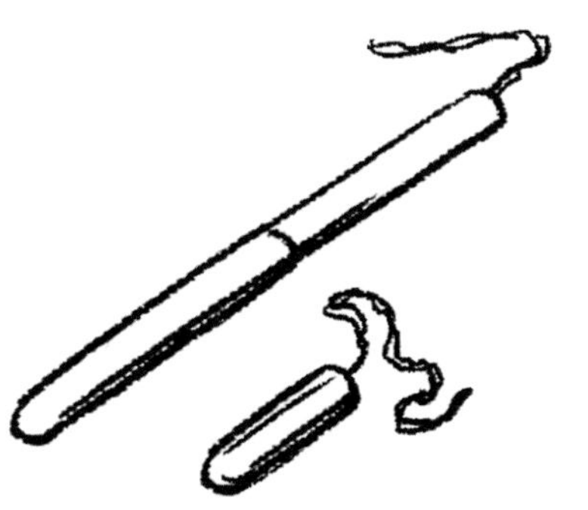

Tampons are small tubes of cotton bought at a pharmacy or store. They are put into the vagina to absorb blood. Tampons have a strong soft cotton string attached to them which hangs down outside of the vagina. To remove a tampon, pull on the string. You should only use one tampon at a time. To avoid infections, you should not wear a tampon for more than six hours at a time. You can use tampons and still be a virgin.

Pre-menstrual syndrome

Some women experience mood swings, cramps and a swollen belly just before or during their periods. Their breasts might feel sensitive and swollen. These are all symptoms of pre-menstrual syndrome. This is normal and is caused by the hormone changes that occur during menstruation.

Some things that women can do to ease the symptoms are:

- keeping active
- eating well
- drinking plenty of water
- deep breathing
- rubbing the lower tummy and back
- taking painkillers like Panadol.

Activity 4·2 KNOW YOUR CYCLE!

Each woman's body is different. It is very important for you to get to know your menstrual cycle and what is 'normal' for you. This will also help you to make sure you have sanitary pads or other methods ready to avoid accidents.

Keep a diary for three months.

1 How often do you get your periods?
2 How long do your periods last?
3 Do you experience mood swings, swelling, bloating or other pre-menstrual syndrome symptoms? Do these happen before your period? During your period?
4 Can you predict which date your period will start on?

Compare your diary with your friends' diaries.

Supporting your breasts

During puberty, girls' breasts will start to grow. At a certain point, it may become uncomfortable for you to move around and run. You should consider starting to wear a bra. Throughout puberty, a girl may need to get a different-sized bra every couple of years, as her breasts continue to grow.

Sexual feelings and response

It is normal for girls to start to experience sexual feelings and responses. Throughout puberty a girl's clitoris, nipples and other places on her body will become more sensitive to touch. She will be able to have an orgasm (extreme sexual excitement). Her vagina will become wet with a clear fluid when she is excited. Some girls may have sexually arousing dreams as they go through puberty. These dreams may continue when they are adults. All of these responses are normal. They are a healthy part of becoming an adult and discovering sexuality and sexual feelings.

Being the centre of attention

Girls usually begin puberty before boys. For girls in school and in the community, growing taller, having breasts and starting periods can draw attention from boys and older men. This can be uncomfortable.

You have the right to be protected and safe from sexual comments in your home, school and community. If you feel threatened or uncomfortable with how a man is speaking to you or touching you, get help from a trusted adult immediately.

Signs of problems with your body

Most of a woman's reproductive system is hidden away inside her body. This makes it difficult for a woman to know if there is something wrong. A woman should speak to a health worker if:

- she has not had her first period by the time she is 17 years of age
- she has a very painful period, or if there is heavier bleeding than usual during her period
- her vagina has a particularly strong smell, or if there is yellow or green fluid coming from the vagina
- there are sores on her labia or inside the vagina
- she misses her period (there are many reasons for a woman to miss a period, such as stress, weight loss, sickness, pregnancy and breastfeeding).

These are all common situations. Usually, the cause of these problems can be diagnosed and treated easily by a health worker. If you experience any of these problems, see your health worker as quickly as possible.

Keeping your reproductive system healthy is important for your overall health, and also if you plan to have children.

Activity 4·3 CAMPAIGN

If you are an older girl who has had her period for a few years, what can you do to help girls younger than you?

1 Talk to younger sisters, friends and family members. What do they know about periods? Do they have any questions or concerns?

2 With peers, plan and carry out an advocacy campaign aimed at your community or school about puberty and menstruation to help improve support and services for girls. Try to include practical ideas (for example, campaigning to make sure the school shop has homemade and commercial sanitary pads or campaigning for more girls' toilets).

3 What do you think boys and young men should know about women's puberty and menstrual cycles? Include messages for boys in your campaign.

Chapter 5 A boy's guide to healthy puberty

Boys usually begin puberty at a slightly older age than girls. Not all the physical changes happen at once and each man develops slightly differently. For example, some men grow a thick beard and chest hair and others don't.

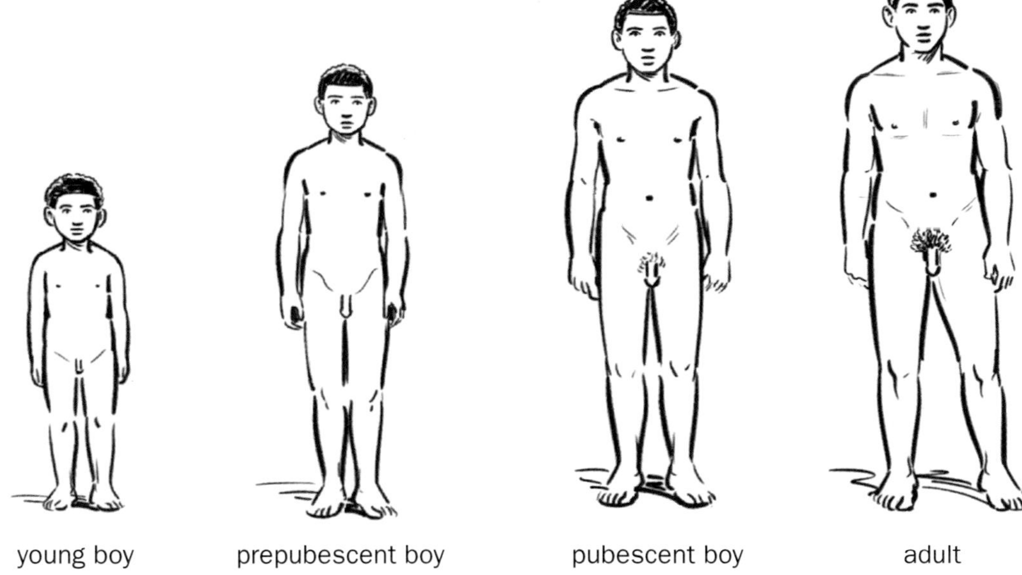

young boy prepubescent boy pubescent boy adult

These are some of the physical changes that happen to a boy during puberty:

- His height increases and shoulders broaden.
- His voice deepens.
- Pubic hair grows at the base of the **penis** and on the **scrotum**.
- His body hair increases (e.g. under the arms, on the face and chest).
- The penis, testes and scrotum grow larger.
- The testes begin to produce sperm and **semen** and the boy is able to **ejaculate**.
- Wet dreams and erections begin.
- He develops sexual feelings and the ability to orgasm.

Boys need to understand their reproductive systems and how to keep them healthy. They should not feel shy or embarrassed to learn about the different parts of the reproductive system.

Male reproductive system

Unlike the female reproductive system, most of the male reproductive organs are outside of the body. This makes it easier for young men and boys to examine them and keep them healthy.

The internal male reproductive organs

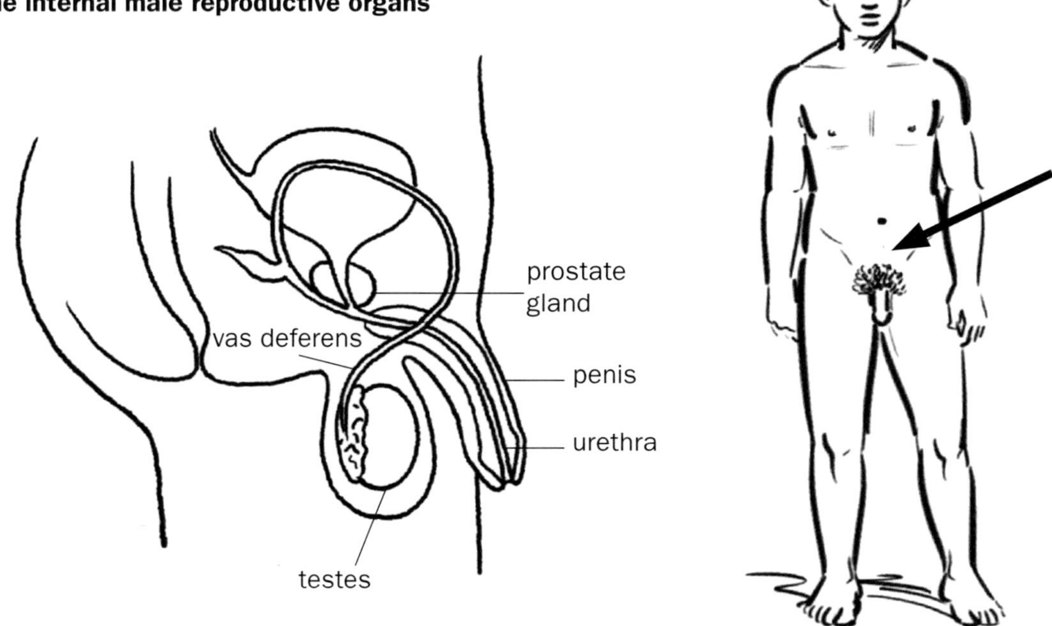

The functions of the parts of the male reproductive system are listed in the Glossary at the back of the book.

The external male reproductive organs

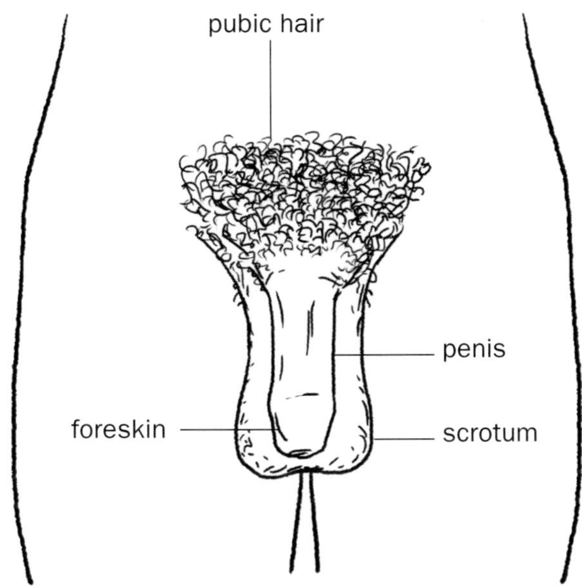

You can read more about the reproductive system in the *Health for the Pacific: Body Systems* book.

 Changes in the reproductive organs

Some of the physical changes include getting erections, starting to ejaculate and having wet dreams. All of these events are a normal part of being a man.

Erections

When a male has an erection, his penis fills with blood and becomes hard and straight. Men usually get erections when they are sexually excited.

Men and boys can also have erections when they are not sexually excited. During puberty, adolescent males may get erections for no apparent reason and when they least expect it. This happens because of the changing hormone levels in a developing boy's body.

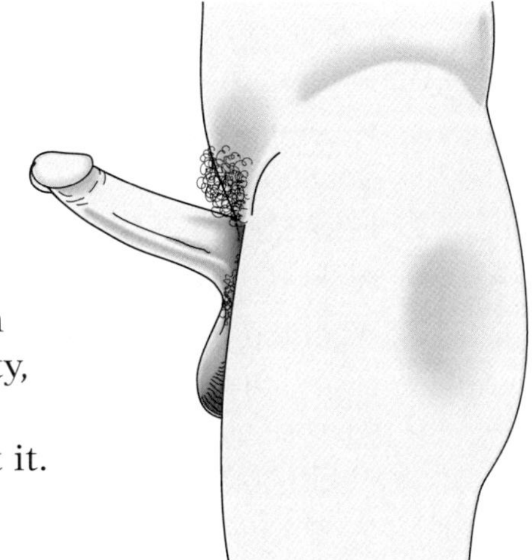

With time, these unexpected erections will stop. It is also common for men and boys to wake up with an erection in the morning.

Ejaculation

If a man becomes very sexually aroused (usually by rubbing the penis) he will **ejaculate**. Sperm from the testes is mixed with a white fluid called semen and pumped out of the erect penis in quick, short bursts. This is the male orgasm.

A man does not ejaculate every time he has an erection. If he waits, his erection will go down on its own.

When a boy starts to produce sperm during puberty, he is able to fertilise an egg and create a baby. If the sperm is ejaculated into a woman's vagina during sexual intercourse, she may become pregnant.

However, this does not mean that he is emotionally, mentally, or socially ready to start having sexual relationships or to become a father. There are still many things that a boy must learn and experience before he is mature enough to have a relationship or raise a family.

Activity 5·1 TALK TO YOUR BROTHERS, FATHER AND UNCLES

All men go through puberty.

Talk to your family and older peers about their experiences.

1. How old were they when they first started puberty?
2. How did they feel?
3. What did they experience?
4. What did they wish they knew before puberty began?
5. What advice do they have for you to keep safe and healthy?

Wet dreams

During puberty, when boys start to ejaculate, they may also start to have wet dreams. A wet dream is when a boy or man has a sexual dream and ejaculates in his sleep.

Boys cannot control whether or not they have wet dreams. Some boys have wet dreams often while other boys rarely have wet dreams. Both of these situations are normal.

Circumcision

Penises can be either circumcised or uncircumcised. All men are born with a foreskin protecting the tip of their penis. Some boys and men have their foreskin cut away. This can be for cultural, personal or medical reasons. Circumcision should always be done by an experienced health worker using a sterile blade to prevent infection.

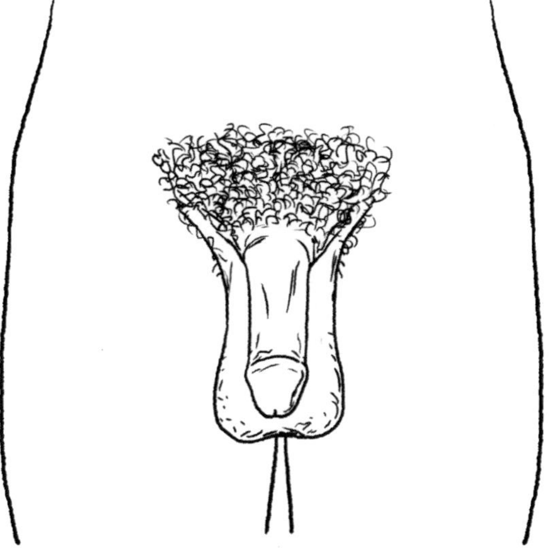

Some men experiment with other kinds of cutting and inserting objects under the skin of the penis. This increases the risk of infection and can seriously damage the penis.

Risk taking

As boys go through puberty they are exposed to more peer pressure. Alcohol, drugs and violence are high risks for young men. They might be pressured to have risky sex or pay for sex. They could be vulnerable to cults in school.

It is important that all young men learn how to deal safely with these risks and respect their health and their community.

Activity 5•2 BEING A PEER EDUCATOR

A peer educator is a young person who is a good role model for behaviour and who knows accurate information about puberty and sexuality.

1 Is there a peer education program in your community? Who runs it? How do they select their peer educators?
2 How could you help your peers to stay healthy and safe during puberty?
3 What advice would you give to your younger brothers?

Personal hygiene

It is important for young men to keep themselves clean so that they stay healthy. Young men should wash their entire body, including the penis, scrotum and **anus**, with soap each day. If they have not been circumcised, they should take care to gently pull back the foreskin and wash underneath it around the head of the penis. Eating healthily will help their body grow well.

Signs of problems with your body

If you experience any of these symptoms, see your health worker as quickly as possible:

- unpleasant smells and discharge from your penis
- sores or boils on your scrotum or penis
- pain when ejaculating or urinating.

Most of these situations are treatable. Keeping your reproductive system healthy is important for your overall health, and also if you plan to have children.

Chapter 6 Healthy sexuality

Sexuality is a very important part of being a human being. It is made up of many parts.

Our sexuality develops and changes through our lives. Desires can change as we get older. There are also many influences on sexuality. Some of these are presented below.

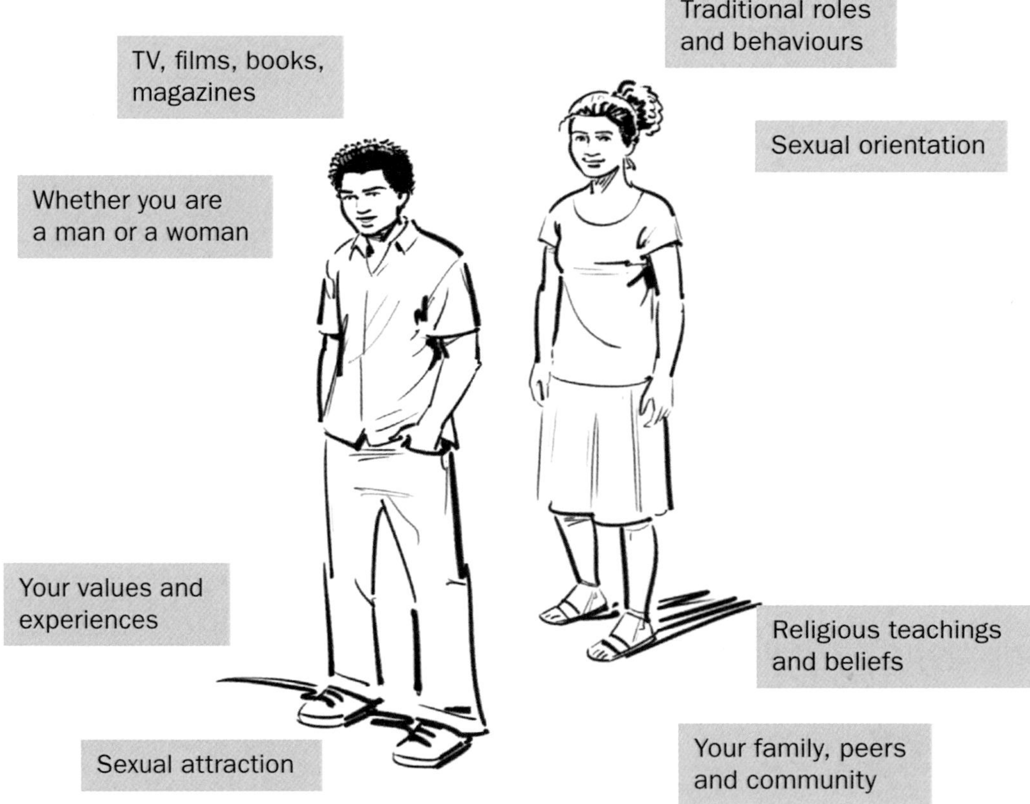

Sexuality is very complicated and each of us develops our own sexuality. It will guide how we behave towards others, especially people we are attracted to. Sexuality can be a source of pleasure, intimacy and comfort and a way of expressing love and affection. It is an important part of our lives.

Sexuality in our lives

Your sexuality can influence your decisions, how you think and how you behave.

How we think and feel	How we act and behave
Who and what we find sexually attractive	How we act and behave towards others
How we feel about sex, romance and desire	How we are expected to behave

We can show our sexuality in many ways, such as through our behaviour, how we dress, and our relationships. However, it is important to remember that we do not always have to act on our private thoughts, desires and feelings. We can still make responsible decisions.

Sexual orientation

People are attracted to either the opposite sex or their own sex or sometimes both. A person's sexual orientation becomes obvious during puberty.

Homosexual	Sexually attracted to the same sex
Heterosexual	Sexually attracted to the opposite sex
Bisexual	Sexually attracted to both sexes

A person's sexual orientation is something they are born with. Your sexual orientation is a natural part of who you are.

Young men and women can sometimes worry about their sexual orientation and their strong sexual feelings towards others. These emotions are a normal part of becoming an adult. It is important to respect your own body, and to show understanding, respect, empathy and tolerance to others.

Being a man, being a woman

In many cultures men and women are expected to behave differently. Sometimes these behaviours are healthy but sometimes they can be harmful.

What harm could these behaviours cause?

Girls and boys, women and men are often given different roles and responsibilities when they reach puberty.

What harm could these behaviours cause?

Sexuality and sexual relationships are also influenced by culture. Sometimes these rules can be harmful to people, especially women and girls.

What harm could these attitudes cause?

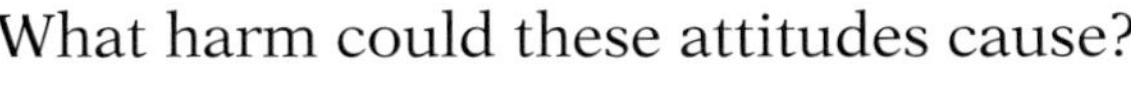

It is important to change cultural attitudes which harm the development and health of young people. It is the responsibility of everyone in the community, including the young men and women themselves.

Activity 6·1 DOUBLE STANDARDS?

A 'double standard' is when the same rules do not apply to both men and women. Double standards are common with sexual behaviour, when men are expected to behave differently to women.

What do you think about the two statements above?
How are the behaviours being judged?

Messages about sexuality

We get many of our values and attitudes from our peers, family, church and community. We also get different messages about sexuality from a wide range of sources. These sources include:

- our traditional culture
- our religion and beliefs
- modern society
- peers
- family
- the laws we live by
- media such as television, magazines, pornography, music, advertisements, etc.

Some of these messages are positive and healthy, but some can be harmful.

Activity 6·2 DISCUSSION

With a group of mixed peers discuss these questions.

1. Which of these sources *most* influences how you think about sexuality?
2. Which sources are the most *positive* influences? Why?
3. Which sources are the most *negative* or harmful influences? Why?

Activity 6·3 WHAT MESSAGES DO YOU GET ABOUT SEXUALITY?

These are some of the different ways some people show their sexuality.

Clothes

Marriage

Who we find attractive

Holding hands

Flirting

Dancing

Kissing

Sexual practices

Who we think makes a good partner

Behaviour towards the same and opposite sex

Pornography

Raising children

Choose one or more behaviours and complete a table that compares what each source says about that behaviour. For example:

	Peers	Traditional culture	Church	TV and magazines
Messages for girls				
Messages for boys				

Healthy and unhealthy sexuality

Having a positive and healthy sexuality will allow you to have a happy and healthy life, relationships and family. Healthy sexuality includes having a respectful and equal relationship with your partner.

Sexuality and culture

Many cultures in PNG have interesting ways of demonstrating sexuality and adulthood.

Trobriand Island dancing

Manus dancing

Huli wigman

Negative sexuality happens when one partner has power or control over another partner. The partner does not respect their partner's values. It can lead to emotional, physical and in some cases sexual abuse. This can be very harmful to relationships and families.

Pornography

Watching pornographic films or looking at pornographic pictures is something many young people do. Pornography can be arousing but it can also give harmful messages about sexual practices and attitudes towards women. It is illegal in Papua New Guinea and banned in schools.

Chapter 7 Love, relationships and marriage

During adolescence, the relationships young people have with their families, friends and community will start to change. For the first time, many young people begin to have romantic relationships.

It is helpful to understand the differences between the kinds of relationships that can form as adolescents and adults.

 Friendship

Friendships become increasingly important for young people as they become more independent. In some traditional cultures, strong friendships with the opposite sex would be considered unusual, but this attitude is changing.

Peer groups will form. This is normal, but peer groups should be positive and supportive. If people are bullied or excluded from peer groups, or if the peer group forces them to take risks or behave badly, this can be very harmful.

Friendships built on respect, trust, shared interests, good communication and positive values can last a lifetime.

Activity 7·1 PEER PRESSURE CASE STUDY

Hannah was in Grade 8. She was a successful student and was popular. Her group of female friends were always together: in class, after school, and on the PMV home. They shared all their secrets. After the final Grade 8 exam they bought a bottle of home brew off some older boys, headed into town and started drinking. Hannah had promised her mum she would be home early... but she wasn't.

1 What were the positive benefits of Hannah's peer group? What were the harmful effects of her peer group?
2 Why do you think Hannah went drinking with her friends?
3 What could be the consequences of Hannah's behaviour?
4 What would a better friend have said to Hannah to prevent her getting into trouble?
5 If you were Hannah, what would you have said?
6 Now write five rules for positive peer groups. For example, 'respect the right to say "no"'.

Sexual attraction

Being sexually attracted to someone is a powerful feeling most young people experience. However, we are not all attracted to the same features!

For example, attractiveness can include:

- what the person looks like (eyes, face, body, clothes)
- how they move
- what they say
- how they behave
- how they think
- their values
- their work.

Who we find attractive is part of our sexuality and it is unique. It also changes over time. The type of person you are attracted to now may not be the type of person you are attracted to when you are older.

When someone feels sexually attracted to another person, their body reacts. They can become aroused. For young people these strong feelings can be very confusing and can lead to shyness or acting foolishly. Again, it is important to remember we don't have to act on our feelings.

Infatuation

Infatuation is being so attracted to one person that the feelings and desire become almost all you think about. Adolescents and adults sometimes confuse infatuation with love. Infatuation is a natural feeling that is often found at the beginning of a sexual relationship. Infatuation can fade, which makes it a difficult emotion to deal with.

Infatuation can be exciting and harmless but it can sometimes cause trouble and lead to poor decision-making.

For example, if you are infatuated with a boyfriend you may agree to have sex and even marry him. Then, once the infatuation wears off, you may discover he has many faults. There is a danger of ending up in an unhealthy or abusive relationship.

Love

There are many different types of love: love between a husband and wife, love for your children, love for God, love for friends, love for your country. There have been thousands of songs, poems and stories written about love because it is such an important emotion.

Intimate love between two adults is more than sex and more than sexual attraction. The love between a couple can develop and grow over many, many years. Desire, intimacy, trust and respect are all part of developing love between partners.

Some people fall in love with just one person in their life. Others may fall in love several times. Like human sexuality, love is a complex emotion.

Changing relationships

As young people start to experience different sexual and romantic feelings, their relationships may also start to change.

Having a boyfriend or girlfriend

Having a boyfriend or girlfriend is an exciting time for a young person. It gives you the chance to get to know someone, explore sexuality and learn how intimate relationships work. It is important that you respect the rules of your school, family and traditional culture when dating.

Be sure to think about your decision and remember that you don't have to act on your feelings. Here is some good advice for healthy and safe dating.

- ☑ Be clear about your rules: if you are not sure, say 'no'.
- ☑ Keep yourself safe. Avoid being alone in unsafe places. If you have sex, make sure it is safe sex.
- ☑ Treat your boyfriend or girlfriend in the same way you expect to be treated; do not pressure them.
- ☑ Be honest.
- ☑ If you want to split up with your boyfriend or girlfriend, be honest, clear and positive.
- ☑ Ask for relationship advice from a trusted adult if you are worried.

Marriage

Marriage and having children are often two long-term goals for young people. A healthy marriage is a partnership based on love, trust, respect and good communication. Sharing responsibilities for family life helps create a successful marriage. Intimacy and a healthy sexual life are also important.

It is healthy to think carefully about marriage before you get married.

- How would you like to be treated?
- Would this person treat you that well?
- Are you old enough and ready for a lifelong commitment?
- Are you in love or just infatuated?
- Do you feel pressure to be married?

Discussing future marriage with trusted friends, family and church workers is a good idea. Marrying too young, before you have completed your education, for example, could lead to problems. Marrying the wrong person (such as someone who is violent or neglectful) could be very risky.

The *Health for the Pacific: Healthy Relationships* book explores intimate and romantic relationships in more depth.

Chapter 8 Sexual intercourse and sexual pleasure

Both men and women can give and receive sexual pleasure. Sex between two people who love, respect and trust each other is very intimate and special. Most people will have sex in their lives so it is important that adolescents do not rush into having a sexual relationship. Waiting until you are older and more in control of your emotions may be safer and healthier.

Sexual relationships always come with responsibilities and consequences.

It is important to think about the possibility of a sexual relationship *before* you have sex.

Why do people have sex?

People choose to have sex for different reasons. For example:

- to have children
- for pleasure
- to share love and feel intimacy.

However, some reasons for having a sexual relationship are unhealthy:

- because you are forced to
- to show off
- for money or food.

Stop! In the name of love!

Abstaining from sex when you are young is perfectly normal and will keep you safe and healthy. Never feel pressured into having sex. You might want to wait until you are older or married.

You can have a boyfriend or girlfriend without having sex.

Even once you have had sex you can still choose to abstain later.

Activity 8•1 GOOD CHOICE OR POOR CHOICE?

- With a partner, brainstorm good and poor reasons for starting a sexual relationship when you are still an adolescent. For example:

Good reasons for starting a sexual relationship	Poor reasons for starting a sexual relationship
To start a family	Because you were drunk
Because you are married	All your friends said they were having sex

- Next, examine each of these reasons again. Which of them would change if you were older or married? Why?

Consequences of sex

Starting a sexual relationship when you are too young can be emotionally harmful and risky to your health. There can be serious consequences from this behaviour.

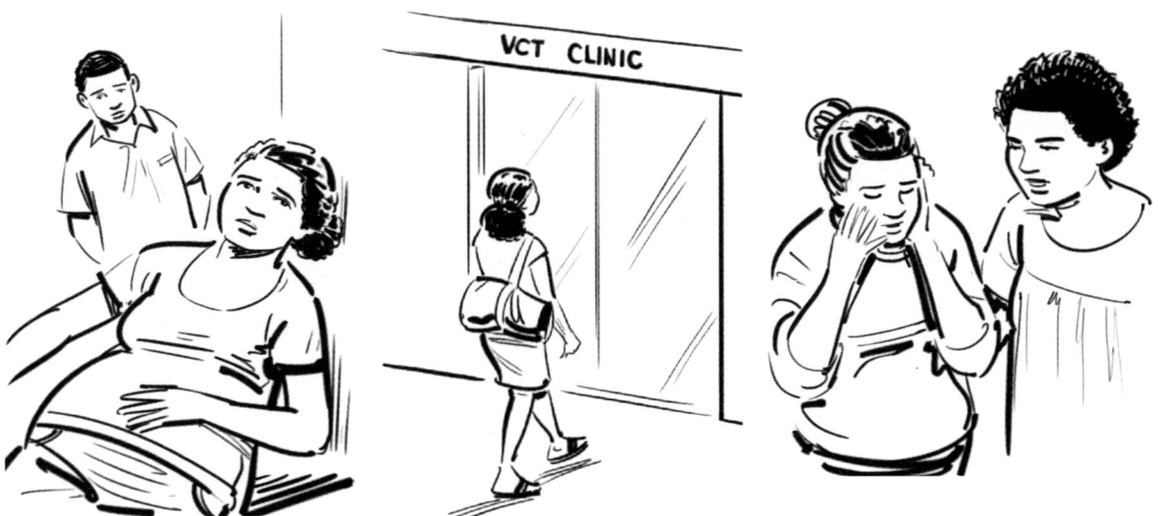

Unplanned pregnancy

Infection with HIV or another STI

Emotional upset and conflict

Activity 8·2 WHAT ARE YOUR GOALS ABOUT SEXUAL RELATIONSHIPS?

It is important to make your own decisions about sex and sexual relationships. Consider the following questions to help you learn what is right for you.

1 When is the right time in life to start a sexual relationship? Why?
2 How will you decide that you are old enough for a sexual relationship? What age or stage of life would be right for you?
3 What do you aim to achieve before then?
4 How will you protect the health of yourself and your partner?
5 What is your main reason for not having sex when you are too young?

Sexual responsibility

Responsible and healthy sex is:

- wanted by both partners
- private
- in a loving, trusting and strong relationship
- pleasurable
- safe from unplanned pregnancy, STIs and HIV
- based on good communication.

No one should ever be forced or bullied into having sex. Responsible sex does not break the values of either person. For many people, this means that sex takes place within a marriage or a long-term stable relationship.

Remember that we do not need to have sex just because we have sexual feelings and desires. We can enjoy those feelings without putting ourselves at risk.

Sexual intercourse

Sexual intercourse is also known as 'sex' or 'making love'. There are also many slang or vernacular words to describe it. Some of these words are rude in the community and in school.

It is important that you understand what sexual intercourse is to help you make safe and healthy decisions.

The physical stages of sexual intercourse are:

1 Sexual attraction and dating

2 Foreplay

Talking to, kissing, touching, hugging each other

3 Sexual intercourse and orgasm

4 Relaxation and sleep

Relaxing, sleeping, talking and feeling close and loving

What is foreplay?

Foreplay is sexual touching, hugging, talking and kissing. The couple's heart rate and breathing increases and their bodies start to become sexually aroused. They feel strong emotions and desires.

Sexual response in women

- vagina becomes wet and slippery
- clitoris becomes more sensitive
- labia swell
- nipples harden

Sexual response in men

- penis becomes erect and sensitive
- penis produces a clear slippery liquid
- nipples harden

Both men and women can experience an orgasm because of the excitement from rubbing the penis or clitoris. An orgasm is a feeling of intense sexual pleasure.

Some couples stop at foreplay because they do not want to risk an unplanned pregnancy or HIV.

Masturbation

Masturbation is rubbing and stroking the penis, vagina and clitoris to feel sexual pleasure.

Almost all adolescents and adults masturbate and so do many couples. It is a normal and private way of exploring sexual pleasure.

It is also a safe and healthy way of feeling sexual pleasure without risking pregnancy or STIs and HIV.

What are the different kinds of sexual intercourse?

The most common forms of sexual intercourse are **vaginal sex** and **oral sex**. The other kind of sexual intercourse is **anal sex**. It is important to know the health risks of each of these kinds of sex.

Couples will explore each other's needs and desires and often experiment with different kinds of sexual behaviour. Good communication and safe sex are both very important.

Vaginal sex

Vaginal sex is when the man's penis enters a woman's vagina. It is important to make sure the vagina is wet enough so the man does not hurt the woman.

If the man orgasms, he will ejaculate sperm inside her vagina. This can lead to fertilisation and pregnancy.

If the man and woman do not use a condom there is a risk of pregnancy or transmission of STIs or HIV.

Oral sex

Oral intercourse is kissing, licking and sucking the clitoris and labia or penis.

Oral sex does not lead to pregnancy, and the risk of HIV transmission is low, but other STIs can still be passed this way.

Anal sex

Anal sex is when the penis enters the anus. This is a more risky kind of sex for STIs and HIV transmission because the anus can tear and bleed. Using lubricant and a condom reduces the risk to both partners.

During sex it is possible for both men and women to orgasm, depending on their feelings, their experience and how aroused they are.

After having sex, couples will often sleep and relax together. Orgasm releases hormones that make couples feel close and loving towards each other.

Questions young people ask about sexual intercourse

It is natural to be curious about sexuality and sexual intercourse as these are important parts of being an adult. In the past there were many taboos and barriers to young people finding out the right information about their bodies. However, everyone has the right to know the facts about sexuality so they can grow and develop into healthy adults.

Finding a trusted source of accurate information is important. Chapter 12 discusses this in more detail.

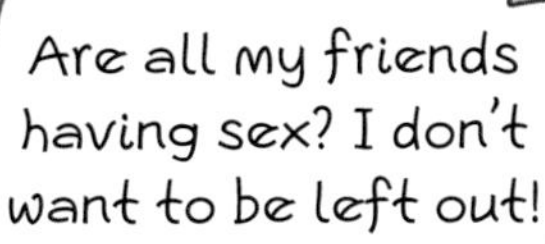

It is important that *you* decide when you want a sexual relationship. This decision should be based on what you know about healthy and responsible sexuality, your feelings and your values.

You have the right to say 'no' to sex and wait until you are older and ready.

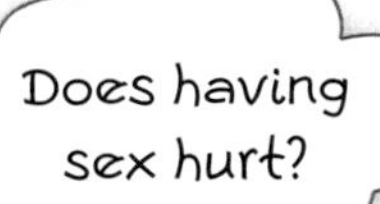

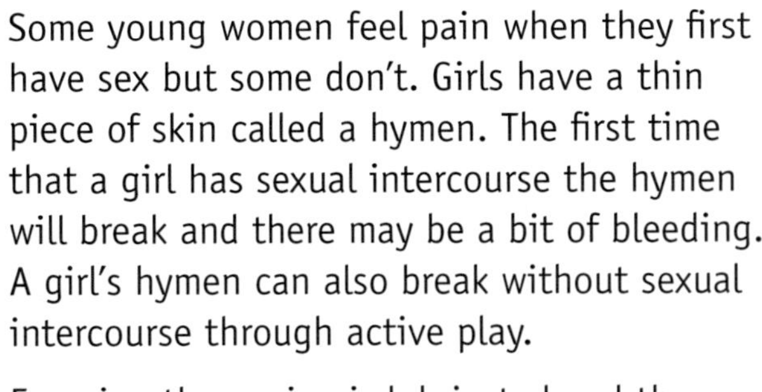

Some young women feel pain when they first have sex but some don't. Girls have a thin piece of skin called a hymen. The first time that a girl has sexual intercourse the hymen will break and there may be a bit of bleeding. A girl's hymen can also break without sexual intercourse through active play.

Ensuring the vagina is lubricated and the woman is aroused is important.

Having sex when the vagina is dry can increase the risk of transmitting STIs and HIV.

Yes, there is a chance she will become pregnant, especially if the man ejaculates inside her.

Using a male or a female condom correctly or using another reliable family planning method reduces the risk of an unplanned pregnancy.

Sex is a special and important emotional moment. It is important for you to decide when the time is right for you to start having sex. Think about:

- your values and beliefs
- whether this is the right person
- whether you need to be married
- how you will feel afterwards
- what the consequences might be
- whether you are under pressure.

If you are not sure, say 'no'.

Activity 8·3 QUESTION BOX

With a same-sex peer, write at least five questions you think boys or girls would ask about sexual intercourse. Put these into a Question Box and collect all the questions from the class.

Pull out the questions one by one and discuss which trusted adult would be the best one to answer the question accurately. Find out the answer and display it in the classroom.

Chapter 9 Safe and healthy sex

Sex should be a responsible, safe and healthy experience. Everyone is responsible for preventing unplanned pregnancies, STIs and HIV. Just because a young person can have sex does not mean they have to have sex. Abstaining from sex or waiting until you are older is a good way of keeping safe and healthy.

It is important to think about whether you are ready for a sexual relationship. This will be different for each person. Use the checklist below to help you think about sexual relationships. This may help you to understand how you feel.

'Am I ready?' checklist

- ❑ Am I *really* ready to have sex? Do I need to be married?
- ❑ Is my boyfriend or girlfriend *really* ready to have sex?
- ❑ What are my reasons for having sex?
- ❑ Am I under pressure? Am I forcing someone else to have sex with me?
- ❑ How will my parents and friends feel about me having sex? Will I have to lie afterwards? Will I feel guilty?
- ❑ What about my moral and religious values about sexuality and love? What does my church say about sexual relationships?
- ❑ Do I know enough about my own feelings and self-control?
- ❑ Do I know enough correct information about safe and pleasurable sex?
- ❑ How will I feel about myself after I have sex?
- ❑ How will I feel about my partner afterwards?

Deciding when is the right time to start a sexual relationship is an important decision. Most adults have had to make this decision already, so you can always ask a trusted adult what they did and what the consequences were.

 Pressure on young men

Young men often feel peer pressure to start sexual relationships. They might feel they need to boast to their friends and 'prove themselves'. If they are drinking home brew, they may feel pressure to make poor choices.

Some cultures believe it is acceptable for a man to have many sexual partners. These pressures are harmful to young men. They need to learn how to resist this pressure.

 Pressure on young women

Young women may also feel pressure to get involved in sexual relationships. Young women are vulnerable to pressure to have sex when they are young through sexual abuse, rape and threats.

They are vulnerable to early marriage and having sexual relationships with older men ('sugar daddies').

Learning to stay safe and resist pressure to have sex is an important life skill for young women.

Sugar daddies

Sugar daddies are older men who have sexual relationships with younger women and girls.

They have money and power. Sometimes they offer mobile phones, clothes, school fees or other goods for sex.

Being the girlfriend of an older, married man can be harmful and puts you at risk of HIV, unplanned pregnancy and angry family members.

Activity 9•1 KEEPING OUR YOUNG PEOPLE SAFE

With a group of mixed-sex peers, discuss these two questions.

1 How can young people be protected from sexual pressure and risks in these places:
   - school
   - church
   - community
   - family?

2 What are the similarities and differences between the sexual pressures on young men and young women? How are they treated differently?

Healthy, safe and responsible sex

The building blocks for a healthy and safe sexual relationship include:

- strong positive values and morals
- good communication skills, including how to say 'no'
- accurate knowledge about sex
- knowing how to have safe sex
- not having sex with someone much older than you
- self-control
- being in a long-term, happy and equal relationship
- self-respect
- confidence
- high **self-esteem**.

Healthy sexual behaviours

If you are thinking about starting a sexual relationship, or if you are already in one and want to stay safe and healthy, these are some strategies you can use.

Abstinence and delaying sex until you and your partner are ready

Abstinence means not having sexual intercourse with your boyfriend or girlfriend. Abstinence does not carry any risk of pregnancy or STIs.

Most young people practise abstinence. They decide what sexual activities are right for them, or 'how far they will go' with their boyfriend or girlfriend; for example, holding hands, kissing.

Your girlfriend or boyfriend should respect your decision to abstain. If they don't, then they are not a very good partner. You should also respect someone else's decision. Putting someone under pressure to have sex is wrong.

> **Saying 'no' is OK**
>
> Being able to resist pressure to have sex is a good skill. You will need to be 'assertive' and communicate clearly.
>
> For example,
>
> *"No, I don't believe in sex before marriage."*
>
> It is a good idea to practise what you will say before you need to say it.

Outercourse

Outercourse is when you touch, rub and stroke the other person. This can be through their clothes or on their skin. It is a way of feeling sexual pleasure and excitement without the risk of pregnancy or STIs.

It is important to tell your partner which parts of your body they can touch over or under your clothes, and which parts are private.

During outercourse, there is no penetration by the penis.

Avoiding alcohol and marijuana

If you are drunk or have taken drugs you might not make sensible decisions about sex. You could put your health at risk.

Using condoms

If you do have penetrative sex, using a male or female condom reduces the risk of unplanned pregnancy and reduces the transmission of HIV and other STIs. Condoms are widely available and can be used with a water-based lubricant.

Using family planning methods

Family planning methods like the contraceptive pill and contraceptive injection can be used to prevent unplanned pregnancy. However, only condoms prevent infection with HIV and STIs as well as pregnancy. There are many different types of family planning methods which are explained in Chapter 11.

Avoiding 'sugar daddies' and paying for sex

It is important that there is equality and respect in a relationship, especially a sexual relationship. A man who is much older than you will have more power and money. He may have many more sexual partners.

Equality and respect are important in a relationship.

Activity 9·2 YOUR STRATEGIES FOR KEEPING SAFE AND HEALTHY

Reflect on the different strategies for healthy and safe sex.

1 Which strategies might you use? Why?
2 What are your goals for sexual behaviour?
3 What are the biggest risks you face in keeping safe and healthy?

Sexual risk

Different forms of sexual activity can put you at higher or lower levels of risk for transmitting HIV or other STIs. The diagram below presents this risk.

No risk of transmitting HIV or other STIs

Abstaining, outercourse, masturbation, hugging, kissing

Low risk of transmitting HIV or other STIs

Sex using a condom properly

Risk of transmitting HIV or other STIs

Vaginal sex without a condom

Oral sex

High risk of transmitting HIV or other STIs

Anal sex without a condom

Activity 9·3 ROLE PLAY

It is important that you learn how to negotiate safe and healthy sex. How would you say 'no' to unwanted pressure? How would you ask for a condom? How would you talk about where you like to be touched?

With a partner, write short role plays for how to respond assertively and safely to these scenarios.

- Telling your partner where they can touch you
- Saying 'no' to penetrative sex and offering alternatives
- Suggesting a safer kind of sex, such as outercourse
- Asking a trusted friend for a condom
- Asking for advice about safe sex from a trusted adult
- Insisting on using a condom when you are having sex

Barriers to safe sex

There are many reasons why people have unsafe sex:

- too embarrassed to ask for condoms or safer sex
- myths about particular sexual practices
- not having enough accurate information
- forced by partner or peers
- being drunk
- not being able to communicate well about sexuality.

Activity 9·4 WHAT CAN WE DO ABOUT IT?

How can we help young people get the correct information about healthy and safe sex?

Working with a mixed-sex group of peers, design a leaflet. List at least ten strategies that would help improve the sexual health of young men and women; for example, distributing copies of this book translated into Tok Pisin.

Rape and sexual abuse

Rape and sexual abuse are serious crimes in our country. Rape is when a person is forced to have sex (vaginal, oral or anal sex). If you are raped or sexually assaulted:

- Immediately tell a trusted adult.
- Go with them to the health centre.
- Make sure you get Post Exposure Prophylaxis (PEP), which protects against HIV, other STIs and pregnancy.
- Contact your nearest Family and Sexual Violence support centre.
- You may go to the police if you wish the person to be charged, but this decision is up to you. Nobody can force you to go to the police if you don't want to.

Chapter 10 Reproduction, fertilisation and pregnancy

After puberty, boys and girls are physically able to create a baby. Their reproductive systems are fully developed and functioning and can produce children. After puberty, boys and girls become fertile.

 How babies are made

To create a baby, **fertilisation** has to take place. Fertilisation is when a woman's egg and a man's sperm meet and join together.

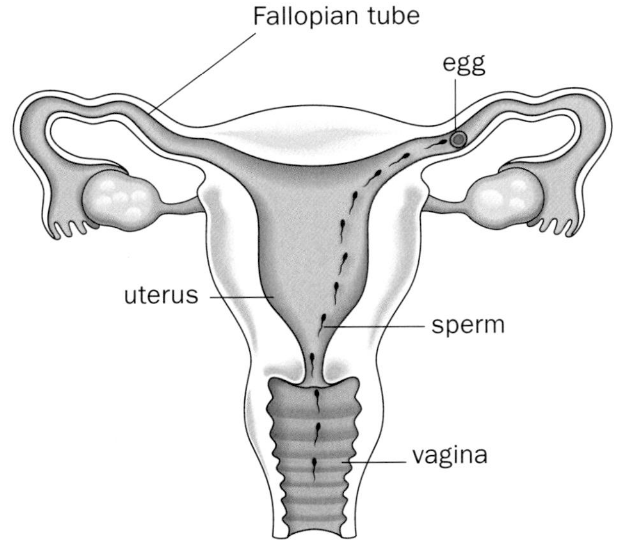

For this to happen, the man and woman have sexual intercourse and the man ejaculates inside the woman's vagina. There are millions of sperm in each ejaculation.

When sperm are in the vagina, they swim through the woman's cervix, into her uterus and then into her Fallopian tubes. Sperm can survive inside a woman's body for more than five days.

If the woman has ovulated recently, an egg will be slowly floating down her Fallopian tube.

Fertilisation happens when one sperm finds an egg and joins with it. Only about 200 sperm will make it as far as the Fallopian tube. Only one of the millions of sperm will fuse with the egg.

Two halves make a whole unique person

A woman's egg contains half of the genetic information that is needed to make a new human being. The other half comes from the man's sperm. When fertilisation takes place, the new cell that is produced has all of the genetic information it needs to grow into a new person.

This is the reason why we sometimes look a little bit like our relatives. We inherit some of our characteristics from our parents, but we are still unique individuals and our bodies will develop in a unique way.

Activity 10·1 WHO DO I LOOK LIKE?

You have inherited some **DNA** from both your father and mother (and some from their parents and their grandparents!).

1 Which family member do you look like?
2 Which features in your face look like someone in your family?

Boy or girl?

The sex of a baby is determined by the DNA in the male's sperm. Half of the sperm cells contain genetic material to make a boy and half of the sperm cells contain genetic material to produce a girl. There is no way to control whether 'male' sperm or 'female' sperm reach the egg first. It is purely chance.

The growing foetus

Soon after fertilisation, the new cell starts to divide and forms a bundle of cells called an **embryo**. The embryo travels down the Fallopian tube and into the uterus, where it will attach to the soft wall lining the uterus. This takes about six days. The place where it attaches will become the placenta.

Once the embryo is implanted in the uterus, it continues to grow and will eventually become a **foetus**. The mother is now pregnant.

Pregnancy

For humans, pregnancy lasts for about nine months. During that time the embryo grows and develops inside a mother's uterus. The growing baby gets all its food, water and oxygen through the placenta from the mother. The placenta sends nutrients and oxygen to the baby and removes any wastes. The umbilical cord is a thick tough tube that connects the placenta to the growing foetus. Your belly button is where the cord was attached to you.

Signs you may be pregnant

When a woman first becomes pregnant there are some changes in her body that she might notice.

- Her periods will stop.
- Her belly becomes larger.
- Her breasts become more sensitive.
- She might get morning sickness.

However, these things can also have other causes. Young women's periods are sometimes irregular, for example.

The most accurate method of finding out whether you are pregnant is a pregnancy test. This can be done at the health centre or with a test kit bought from a pharmacy. Later, the developing baby can be seen on an ultrasound machine at the clinic.

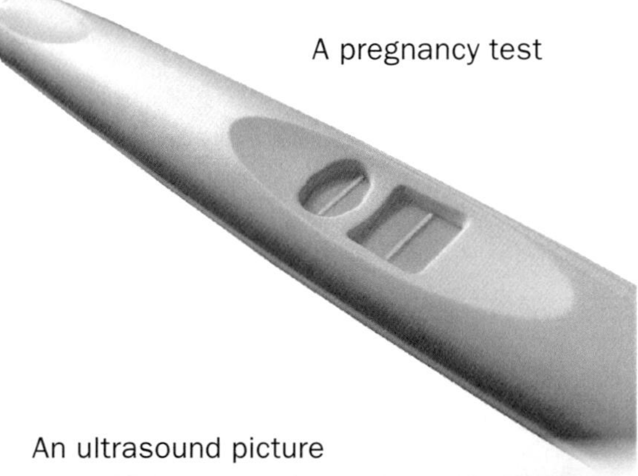

A pregnancy test

An ultrasound picture

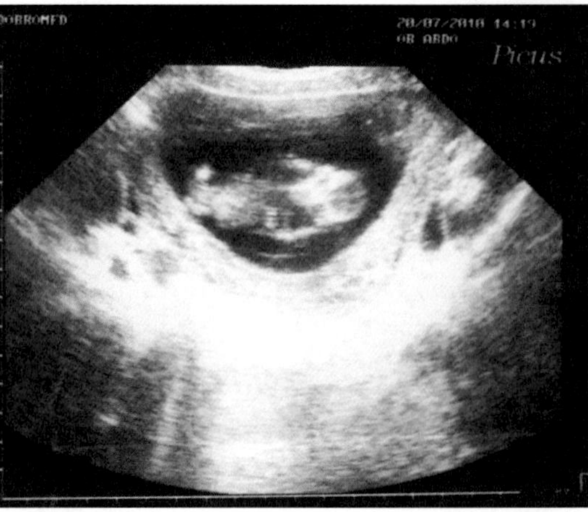

During pregnancy the mother will experience many different changes to her body as the new baby develops. The table below presents some of the changes that happen to the mother and baby during pregnancy.

After three months ...

periods stop
occasional nausea and sickness
mood swings
small bump

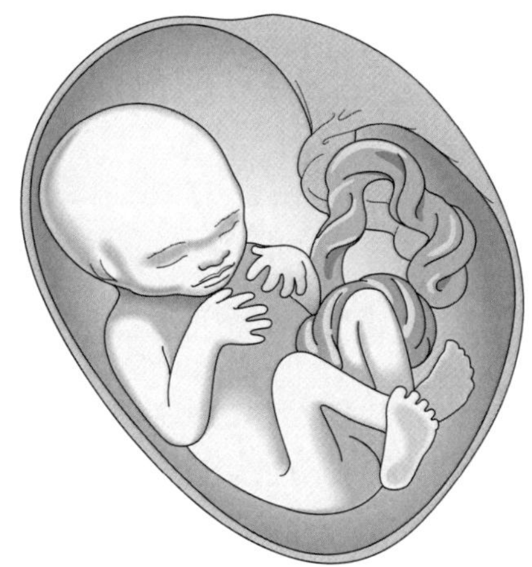

placenta
umbilical cord
brain develops
arms and legs form
heart beats
8 cm long
weighs about 30 g

After six months ...

more energy
sickness stops
belly begins to swell
can feel the baby moving

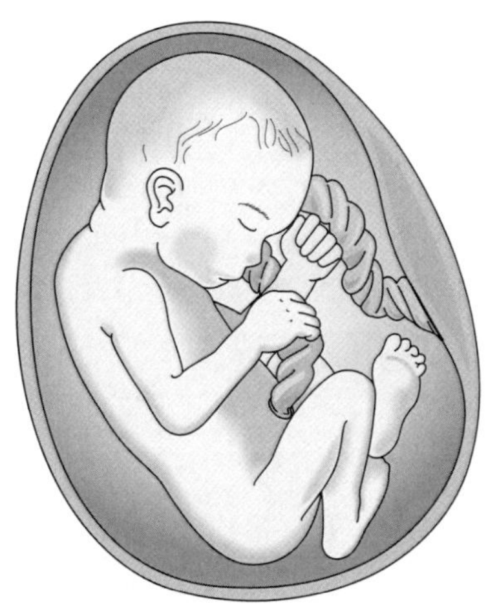

moving in the womb
reproductive organs develop
can hear
sucks thumb
36 cm long
weighs about 800 g

After nine months …

breasts swell
frequent urination
heavy weight causes back aches

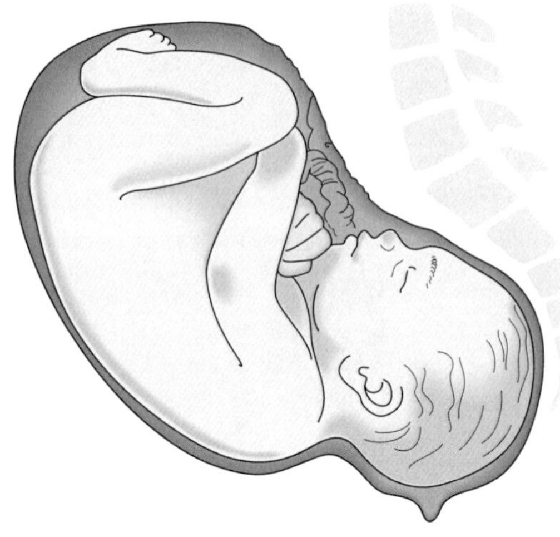

baby very active
grows quickly
ready to be born

over 50 cm long
weighs over 3.5 kg
moves into position for birth

Activity 10·2 INTERVIEW WITH A PREGNANT MOTHER AND FATHER

Design a set of interview questions for a pregnant mother and father in your community. Ask them if they are prepared to be interviewed.

Here are some questions that you can ask:

- How do you feel about having a child?
- What has changed in your life since you became pregnant?
- How do you look after your health?
- What preparations have you begun for your new child?
- If you have other children, how do they feel about the new baby?
- Will the husband be there at the birth?
- Where do you hope to give birth?

Pregnancy can be a very special time for families. It can also be a very difficult time for mothers. Women who are pregnant experience many changes in their bodies as the baby grows and develops. They need care, love and support.

There are some things that women can do to have a healthy pregnancy.

See a health care worker regularly

The health care worker can monitor the growth of the baby and the health of the mother. They can identify if there is anything wrong, provide advice about medicines and help the couple plan for the birth.

Eat a healthy diet

Pregnant women should be sure to eat a healthy diet with plenty of protein, fruit and vegetables, and in particular, leafy greens. The many changes taking place in a woman's body mean that she will need more energy to keep her healthy.

Take care with medicines

Some medicines can be harmful to a growing baby. It is important to tell your health care worker if you are pregnant, so that they can tell you which medicines to take and how much to take so the baby is not harmed.

Avoid alcohol, smoking and other poisons

Chemicals like those found in alcohol and cigarette smoke can be passed from the mother to her baby through the placenta. These chemicals can have harmful effects on the growing baby and the way it develops.

Activity 10·3 ROLES AND RESPONSIBILITIES

Discuss this question with your peers.

What are the responsibilities of the pregnant woman's husband and their community?

Responsibilities of the husband	Responsibilities of their community
For example: • Make sure their home is violence free	For example: • Make sure the health centre is open and properly staffed

Pregnancy and HIV

Pregnant mothers and their husbands will usually be offered an HIV blood test and counselling. If the mother is HIV positive she will be given special anti-HIV medicines called anti-retroviral therapy before and during labour. These reduce the chance of her baby becoming HIV positive. Her baby can also be given anti-HIV medicines when it is born. Because of these medicines, most babies born to mothers with HIV will not be HIV positive.

Healthy labour and childbirth

For most women, labour and childbirth are long and painful, but without complication. However, it is a time when health risks can develop quickly, so it is very important to have a trained health worker present whenever possible. Many women and babies die because there is no midwife or experienced doctor nearby or the families were too slow to get help when the birth did not go well.

What should you do if a woman in your family goes into labour?

- Don't panic.
- Get a trusted female friend to help.
- Make sure the mother is comfortable.
- Inform the health centre midwife.

A sign that a woman is very close to giving birth is when her 'waters break'. This means that the sac in which the baby has been developing has broken and the amniotic fluid comes out of her vagina.

During labour the woman's cervix and vagina stretch. Her uterus contracts. As her contractions become stronger the mother will squeeze her muscles to help push the baby out.

Sometimes, when the baby is being delivered, the vagina and other tissues may tear and there may be some bleeding. In some instances this may require stitches. After the baby is born, the mother will continue to have contractions to force out the placenta and umbilical cord.

When the baby is born the umbilical cord is tied off and cut. The baby should be washed well and wrapped in a clean cloth or blanket. The mother will be very tired for some time, and will need plenty of rest.

Caesarean section

Some mothers have a Caesarean section birth. A doctor cuts a mother's uterus open to remove the baby. This happens in the case of an emergency, or if she has other medical reasons that would make it difficult or dangerous to have a vaginal birth.

Activity 10·4 YOUR BIRTH

1 Interview your mother and father about your birth. Here are some questions you could ask.
   - How long was your mother in labour?
   - What happened during your birth?
   - How did she feel?
   - What did your father do?
   - What did your family do?
   - Where did the birth happen: at home, in hospital or at the health centre?
   - Were you delivered head-first or feet-first?
   - Were you a vaginal birth or a Caesarean birth?
   - How heavy were you?
   - Did you cry or were you quiet?
   - How did your parents feel afterwards?
   - Were you breastfed?

2 Write an autobiography entry for your own birth. For example:

I was born after a short labour of only six hours. This was much less than my brothers and sisters. My mother's waters broke at midnight on the 27th February when she was sleeping in the haus win ...

Healthy early childhood

Once a baby is born there are many things to do. Keeping the baby healthy will help it develop into a healthy and strong child.

It is also important that the mother is cared for and healthy. Giving birth can be exhausting and she will need to eat well and rest.

Breast is best

Breastfeeding is the safest and healthiest way of feeding the new baby. Breast milk is very nutritious and protects the growing baby. It is also clean and free.

Some mothers have to use baby food formula. If they do, they must make sure the water is boiled before making the formula and the bottle is sterilised before each use.

Vaccinations and health checks

Vaccinations protect babies against common diseases. Health workers can tell you which ones are needed and when they will be given.

Health workers can also check that babies are growing properly.

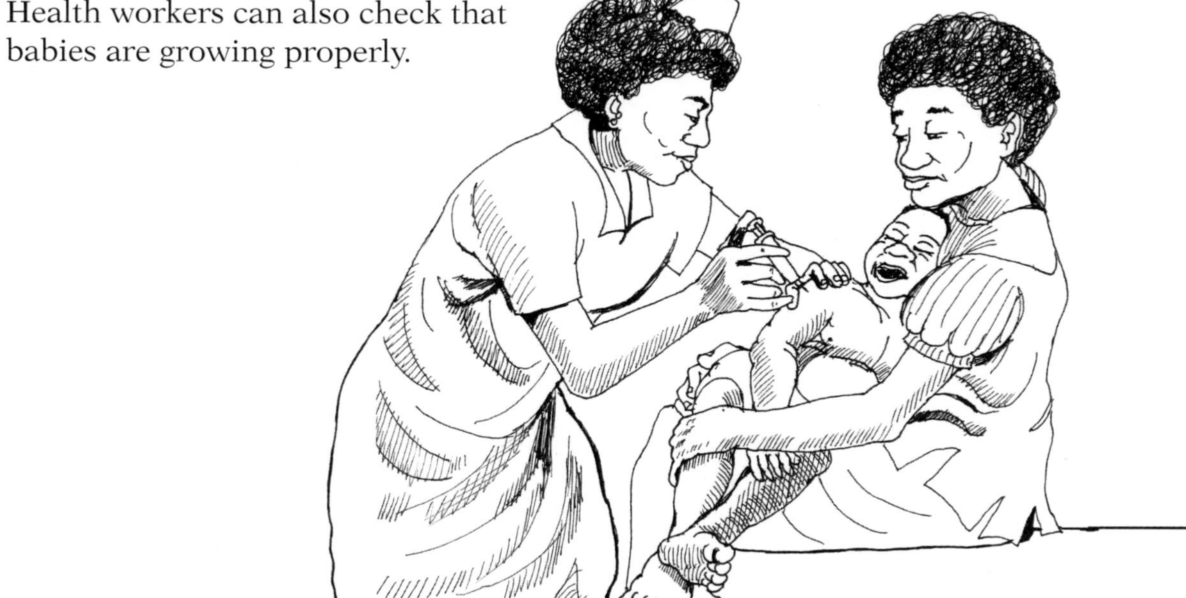

Avoiding malaria and dengue

If a baby is growing up in a place where malaria and dengue are common, they must always sleep under a mosquito net treated with insecticide.

Love and care

Babies need love and care to develop into strong and happy children. Their homes should be free from violence, drugs and alcohol. Their families can help bring up the baby. Changing nappies, cuddling and washing the baby are all things that can be shared.

Chapter 11 Parenthood and family planning

Becoming a parent is an exciting and challenging part of life. It is a lifetime responsibility. Children have a lot of needs that must be provided for by their parents.

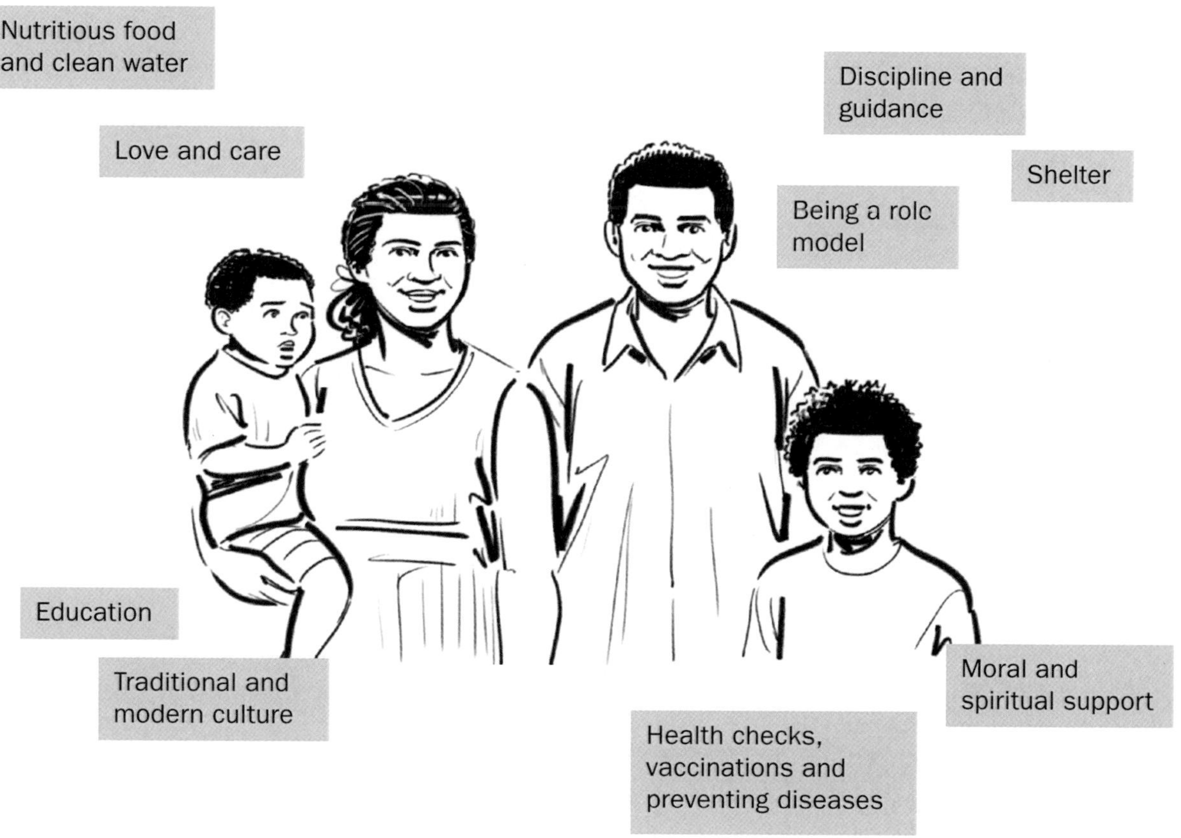

People can become parents in different ways:

- planned pregnancy
- unplanned pregnancy
- adoption.

A planned pregnancy or adoption is far healthier than an unplanned pregnancy.

Becoming pregnant when you are too young can be risky. There are many reasons for this, including the following:

- Young people's relationships may not last or be stable.
- The couple may experience family rejection and conflict.
- They may have to miss out on education.
- There are health risks for pregnant girls aged under 17.

The questions below will help you to think about whether you are ready to become a parent.

Are we ready to be parents?

1. Are we a strong couple who love and respect each other and communicate well? Is our relationship stable and equal?
2. Have we discussed why we want children and when we want them? Do we both want children?
3. Do we have the resources needed to bring up children?
4. Is our home healthy, safe and free from violence and alcohol abuse?
5. Should we be married? Do we have any traditional obligations?
6. Do our families support us having children?
7. Is our health and nutrition good?
8. If we have other children, have we planned a family size we can support and have we spaced our children safely?
9. What will we do if we cannot get pregnant?

Activity 11·1 YOUR ADVICE

With a group of mixed-sex peers, discuss these statements from young people about parenthood. Are these good reasons for getting pregnant? What advice would you give them?

We have been seeing each other since high school. Now my boyfriend is going to university and this is a way I can make him stay loyal to me. We always talked about children anyway.

Our first child was a girl and our second child was also a girl. I need to have a boy to keep our family lands. I am not happy about having more girls.

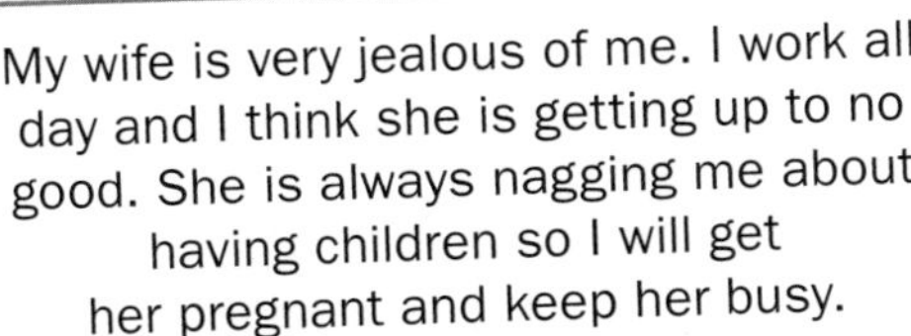

My wife is very jealous of me. I work all day and I think she is getting up to no good. She is always nagging me about having children so I will get her pregnant and keep her busy.

Now write three different scenarios with *good* reasons for starting a family. For example:

'Both my husband and I love children. We have waited until we finished school and started work. We discussed it with our pastor and families. Our house is also finished now so the baby will have a good place to grow up.'

Spacing children

Women who have too many children too closely together risk their health. In Papua New Guinea, for example, far too many women die during pregnancy or childbirth.

Families should space their children using family planning methods.

Activity 11·2 WHAT IS THE BEST SIZE FOR A FAMILY?

Conduct a survey to find out the average family size in your grandparents' generation and your parents' generation.

Now survey how many children your classmates want.

Graph this information. What does it tell you about family size?

Normally, family sizes shrink as people become more educated and have access to family planning services.

What is your opinion about family size? What are the disadvantages of a large family?

Infertility

Some couples cannot have children or take a long time to become pregnant. There are many different reasons why this happens, including untreated STIs, damage to the reproductive organs or ill health. The quality of the sperm and eggs also drops as people get older.

Having trouble getting pregnant is a difficult experience for couples. It is important that their families support them and they get medical advice. If they cannot have children they might be able to adopt.

It is important to keep healthy while trying for a baby. Smoking, drinking alcohol, infectious diseases and poor diet make it harder to have a healthy baby.

Miscarriages

A miscarriage is when the baby dies in the womb before it is born. This can be due to something that is wrong with the developing baby or linked to illness in the mother.

A miscarriage is distressing for the parents and couples should see a health worker if they have repeated miscarriages.

Family planning methods

It is important to protect the health of the woman by spacing children. Most couples use family planning methods to prevent unwanted pregnancies. Used correctly, most family planning methods work very well, although there are advantages and disadvantages to each method.

In most countries, family planning services are free to couples. Some people use more than one kind of family planning method and couples often change the type they use throughout their life.

Family planning method	How it works	Advantages
Male condom	Acts as a barrier to sperm	• Prevents transmission of HIV and STIs
Female condom	Acts as a barrier to sperm	• Stronger than male condor • Prevents transmission of HIV and STIs
Contraceptive pill	Hormone pills taken each day which prevent the woman's body becoming pregnant	• Simple to use • Can also reduce heavy periods • Fertility returns when you stop taking the pills
Contraceptive injection	Hormone injection once every 12 weeks which stops the woman becoming pregnant	• Simple to use • One injection every 12 wee • Protects against cancer of uterus
Inter-uterine device (IUD)	Small device placed in the uterus by a health worker which interferes with the movement of sperm and prevents embryo implantation in the uterine wall	• Does not interfere with sex • Can remain in place for several years
Breastfeeding	Breastfeeding mothers do not produce eggs for approximately the first six months after childbirth	• Natural method • Very healthy for the baby
Fertility awareness	Woman checks her menstrual cycle to see when she is ovulating and when she can have sex safely	• Natural • Helps women know their body
Vasectomy (male sterilisation)	Tying or cutting tubes that the sperm travel along from the testes	• Simple operation • Permanent
Tubal ligation (female sterilisation)	Fallopian tubes cut or tied to prevent the egg reaching the uterus	• Permanent

Disadvantages	How effective it is at preventing pregnancy if used correctly
• Has to be put on before sex	98%
• Has to be inserted into the vagina before sex	95%
• Need to take each day and follow instructions • No protection from HIV and STIs	99.7%
• No protection against HIV and STIs • Fertility returns several months after last injection • Can cause thinning of the bones	99.7%
• Must be fitted by health worker • Can cause bleeding • No protection from HIV or STIs	99.4%
• Does not prevent HIV or STIs Only works: • Until her periods return • When baby only being fed breast milk and no other liquids or foods • For six months	99.1%
• No protection against HIV and STIs • Needs expert instruction • Body changes can be hard to recognise	75–97% (varies depending on skill of the woman)
• Short-term bruising • Needs experienced doctor • No protection from HIV and STIs	99.9%
• Risks from operation • Needs experienced doctor • No protection from HIV and STIs	99.5%

Activity 11·3 DEBATE AND DISCUSSION

With a group of peers discuss these questions.

1 Which family planning methods do you plan to use? Why?
2 Why do young people find it hard to get access to family planning? What can we do to improve this situation?
3 Why is it important that the couple choose the family planning methods together?

Abortion

An abortion is when a pregnancy is ended using special medicines or surgery. Countries have laws saying when and why an abortion can be used; for example, if the mother's life is at risk from the pregnancy or the unborn baby is not developing properly. An abortion is usually done early in a pregnancy.

Any abortion should always be carried out by an experienced doctor. There are serious risks to the woman's life and future fertility if she has an illegal or 'homemade' abortion (for example, by using poisonous herbs).

Abortion is a controversial issue. Some people say the life of the unborn baby must be protected, while others say that women have the right to choose, especially when abortion is needed to protect the life of the woman.

Having an abortion is an emotional and difficult event for couples.

Activity 11·4 TEENAGE PREGNANCY

Case study

Mathias and Elizabeth are both 16 years old and in their final year of primary school. They have both done well in school and both expect to go to secondary school. They have been close friends for many years. Over the past year, their friendship turned into a romantic relationship.

During their holidays, Mathias and Elizabeth decided that they wanted to make love for the first time. It is now a few months later, they have had unprotected sex several times, and Elizabeth has discovered that she is pregnant. Mathias and Elizabeth's families are not pleased about this. They have not been expelled from school but they will have to leave to look after the child.

1. What are the consequences for Mathias? For Elizabeth? Are they the same?
2. How do you think Mathias is feeling? Elizabeth? Are the feelings the same?
3. How will life change for Mathias? For Elizabeth? Are the changes the same?
4. What options do Mathias and Elizabeth have?
5. What could Mathias and Elizabeth have done to avoid this situation?
6. What would you do if you were in this situation?

Chapter 12 Where can I find the right information?

It is natural to want to find out more about sexuality, parenthood and birth. However, some sources of information can be inaccurate.

A trustworthy source of information will tell you if they don't know the answer to your question. They will understand it is normal to be curious about sex and will not be judgmental. They will not embarrass you and you should feel comfortable talking to them.

Talking about sex and sexuality can be difficult, especially if your culture has taboos. However, it is important that your questions are answered accurately. The wrong information might harm your health.

Sources of information could include:

- teachers who have been trained to teach about sexuality
- trained school-based counsellors and guidance officers
- trained peer educators
- textbooks and health leaflets
- special telephone helplines or websites for young people
- health workers
- NGOs which work with young people, like Save the Children
- magazines, films, TV and other media
- peers
- older brothers and sisters, aunties and uncles, parents
- elders and pastors.

If you are not sure about what someone has told you, go and find another trusted source. You have the right to reliable information.

Activity 12·1 WHO WILL YOU ASK?

Think about your local community. Where and from who could you find accurate information about puberty, reproduction and sexuality?

1 Rank the sources of information from the most reliable to the least reliable.

2 List at least three trustworthy sources of information that you will use.

For example:

Name:

Occupation:

Mobile number:

Location:

Why they would be a good source of information:

Activity 12·2 MY PERSONAL GOALS

What are your goals for your own personal development? Reflect on what you will do to keep healthy and safe.

Complete these statements with your own goals.

My role model for healthy sexuality is ________ because ...

In my community and life these things put my sexual health at risk ... and this is what I will do about it ...

If I have a girlfriend or boyfriend I will keep myself and them safe by using these sexual practices ...

I will not have sex until ...

I will go to ________ for advice and support because ...

My future family will be this size ________ because ... and I will use these methods of family planning ...

This is how I want to be treated by any boyfriend or girlfriend ... and this is how I will treat them ...

Good books about personal development

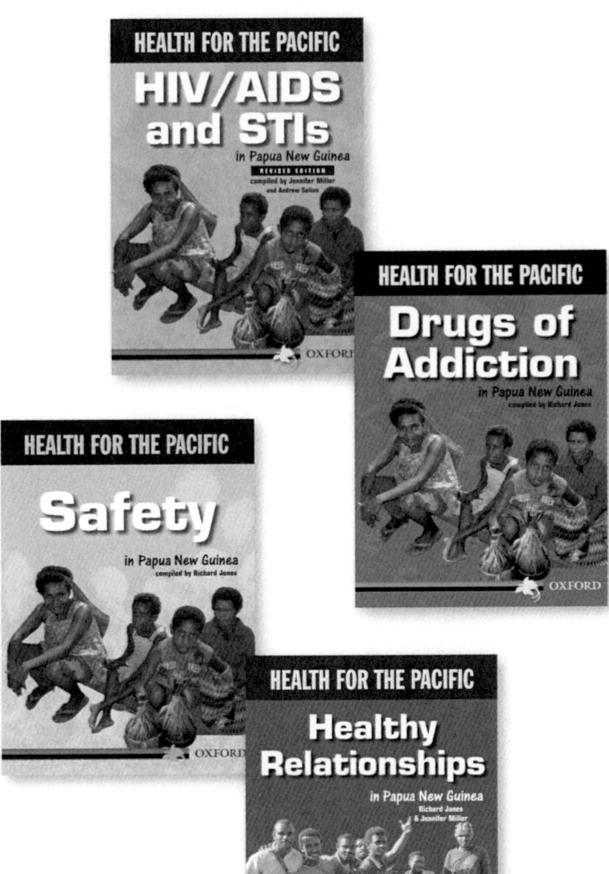

Good websites about sexuality and puberty

Child and teen health information **www.cyh.com**

Family planning information **www.brook.org.uk**

Puberty, peer pressure and sexual health for young people **www.likeitis.org.au**

Accurate health information about sexual practices for young people **www.scarleteen.com**

Accurate information on HIV and STIs **www.avert.org**

Papua New Guinea helplines

Marie Stopes sexual health helpline for young people
8am–10pm, seven days a week, free
7200 5314

BAHA helpline for HIV and AIDS
Seven days a week, free
7200 2242

Organisations who work with young people in PNG

You can find the contact details of these organisations in the phone book or on the internet.

- Save the Children PNG
- Marie Stopes
- Family Health International
- Population Education Project
- UNICEF
- Anglicare StopAIDS
- Childfund
- Pathfinder
- Susu Mama
- Church organisations such as Caritas and ADRA
- Guidance Branch, Department of Education, and all school-based counsellors.

Glossary

abstinence
choosing not to have sex (oral, vaginal, anal) at all

adolescence
the stage of life when young people experience many changes: physical, emotional, intellectual, social. It is the time when children grow and develop into young adults.

anal sex
a form of sexual intercourse where a man puts his penis inside the anus of a woman or a man

anus
part of the human digestive system. It is the body opening through which faeces (poo) comes out.

cervix
part of the female reproductive system. It is the narrow opening between the uterus and the vagina.

clitoris
part of the female reproductive system. It is a small sensitive organ at the top of the vulva on the outside of a woman's body.

DNA
the chemical found in all living things that contains the information on how to make that living thing. The chemical is called deoxyribonucleic acid.

eggs (ova)
female reproductive cells that contain half of the information needed to make a new person. They are stored in women's ovaries. After puberty, one egg is released each month.

ejaculation
when semen comes out of a male's penis during orgasm

embryo
after a woman's egg is fertilised by a man's sperm the new cell will start to grow. Before this bundle of cells reaches the uterus, it is called an embryo. It will eventually develop into a new person.

Fallopian tubes
part of the female reproductive system. These are narrow tubes that lead from the ovaries to the uterus.

fertilisation
when a male's sperm and a female's egg join to make a baby

foetus
once an embryo reaches the uterus and is implanted in the uterine wall it is called a foetus. This will develop into a new person.

foreplay
sexual activity that happens before sexual intercourse: touching, kissing, hugging, stroking and masturbation

foreskin
the skin that covers the head of a man's penis. All boys are born with a foreskin. Some boys have it removed for medical, cultural or traditional reasons.

hormones
chemical messengers

labia
part of the female reproductive system. These are the fleshy lips on the outside of a woman's body that protect the vulva.

masturbation
when a person rubs or strokes their own body parts causing sexual excitement. It is normal and a part of healthy sexuality.

menopause
when a woman stops ovulating (having periods) and she is no longer able to have children

menstruation (period)
when a woman loses a small amount of blood from her vagina. The time from one menstruation to another is called the menstrual cycle. Menstruation is commonly known as a period.

oral sex
when a person uses his or her mouth and tongue to lick or suck a sexual partner's genitals

orgasm
when a man or woman reaches the highest point of sexual excitement. Men will ejaculate and women will feel the muscles in their uterus contract.

ovaries
female reproductive organs which store thousands of eggs. Women have two ovaries.

ovulation
when an egg is released from an ovary. This usually happens once each month,

penis
the male sexual organ. The penis hangs between a male's legs and becomes larger and harder when it is erect.

prostate gland
part of the male reproductive system. Produces semen and acts like a pump to push semen out of the penis when a man ejaculates.

puberty
the period of time when a child matures and develops into an adult (physically, sexually, mentally)

pubic hair
hair that grows around men and women's sexual organs. It starts to grow at puberty.

scrotum
the soft pouch of skin between a man's legs that holds the testes.

semen
the thick liquid that comes out from a man's penis during sex. Semen contains sperm and can carry HIV and other STIs.

self esteem
how a person feels about themselves

sperm
male reproductive cells that contain half of the information needed to make a new person. Sperm are produced in a man's testes and stored in the vas deferens until ejaculation.

testes
part of the male reproductive system. The testes hang outside the man's body in the scrotum. They make sperm cells.

urethra
the tube that passes from the bladder to the outside of a man or woman's body. Urine passes through the urethra to exit the body.

uterus
part of the female reproductive system. It is a strong muscular bag and the place where a baby grows and develops during pregnancy.

vagina
the passage leading from the uterus to the vulva in a female. During sex, a man puts his penis inside the woman's vagina.

vaginal sex
when a man puts his penis inside a woman's vagina

vas deferens
part of the male reproductive system. This is the place where sperm is stored before it is released during ejaculation.

vulva
part of the female reproductive system. This is the name for the external genitals of a woman and includes the labia and the clitoris.